WITH A BOOK
IN MY HAND

WITH A BOOK IN MY HAND

CELIA SUMMER

STEIN AND DAY/*Publishers*/New York

First published in 1977
Copyright © 1977 by Celia Summer
All rights reserved
Printed in the United States of America
Stein and Day/*Publishers*/Scarborough House,
Briarcliff Manor, N.Y. 10510

Library of Congress Cataloging in Publication Data

Summer, Celia.
With a book in my hand.

Includes index.
1. Summer, Celia. 2. Booksellers and bookselling—
New York (City)—Biography. I. Title.
Z473.S895A33   658.8′09′0705730924 [B]   76-47516
ISBN 0-8128-2183-1

For Joan Raines, Igor Kropotkin and
all my friends, past and present, who have
come through the doors of 597 Fifth Avenue

I wish to thank my friends for permission so kindly granted to reprint their letters in this volume.

WITH A BOOK IN MY HAND

Three years ago, a man, a woman, and a boy walked into the Scribner Book Store and passed by me. I spun around abruptly, dropped what I was doing, and blurted out in an astonished tone, "Jesse!"

The man turned toward me and without exchanging a word, we embraced, tears welling in our eyes. I quickly withdrew—the woman with him was probably his equally astonished wife. He introduced us, adding, "and this is our son." I explained to them that Jesse and I had known each other when we were young. I used to be enormously fond of the way he puffed on his delicious-smelling pipe as we discussed his favorite books. We had taken long walks together in Highland Park in Brooklyn, and had been good chums throughout our college years.

Jesse said, "I'm not at all surprised to find you here in a book store, you always loved books most. But what about your father's business?"

I explained that I'd finally left the family's warehouse

With A Book in My Hand

and trucking setup in my brother Harry's hands and was now working at what I really enjoyed. We chatted a while longer, and then said goodbye. I felt nostalgic for those good old irresponsible days. They seemed so far away.

The chance meeting with Jesse triggered the memory of how I arrived at this place where I felt so completely at home. It almost seemed that Celia Summer and books were predestined to become lifelong companions.

It seemed to go way back ... to *Swann's Way* and Bemelmans' *Madeline*. I could hardly concentrate on the hubbub at the store. I sat down on a stool near the south wall bookcases, letting customers pass without asking if they needed help. Jesse would never know how much of the past he had stirred up in me. Those long walks and talks were probably more important than they seemed at the time. "Oh, well," I muttered, "Jesse's right—books were always my compulsion."

I do not remember when my interest in books first started. All I know is that the nicest thing about being one of seven children was that no one ever seemed to know where anyone was; no one ever knew, for instance, the countless hours I spent with my best high-school friend, Bubbles Starfield, lying on her attic floor reading Dorothy Parker, Emily Dickinson, and Edna St. Vincent Millay by candlelight. The friendship provided other advantages, too. Bubbles lived across the street from the library, one block from the tennis courts, and we were able to combine our physical and intellectual pursuits with considerable ease. The fact that I lived twenty blocks away from her was never a deterrent. Walking and bicycling were part of the fun. But most important of all, we were both the youngest of seven sisters and brothers—all in perfectly corresponding order, and so we had infinite bases for comparisons and complaints.

The library, the Arlington branch in Brooklyn, was impressive in every way. On either side of the entrance, a wide stairway led to upper balconies—and now I realize that the Scribner Book Store gives me the same feeling as the library did. I guess I fell in love with both. That library was a home away from home for me. All the goodies were there for the taking, and I feasted.

I also had the good fortune to get a large quantity of beautiful books that were left unclaimed by customers in my father's storage warehouse. They included the eleventh edition of the *Encyclopaedia Britannica*, and complete sets of Flaubert, Balzac, Twain, Poe, Dickens, and both the Continental and Harvard Classics.

I was given wonderful, old-fashioned bookcases with glass doors so that the books did not collect dust the way they do today on open shelves. Although I did not read all these books, I can still recall what they were; I remember there was a novel entitled *I Promessi Spozi* (The Betrothed), and *Dead Souls* by Gogol and countless other classics.

Looking back, I am grateful for the respect for learning instilled in me by my Jewish heritage. Though belligerent at the time at having to study Hebrew, we still had relatives in Europe who expected to receive letters from us. Later, I appreciated this correspondence because

With A Book in My Hand

I am now able to converse with Yiddish-speaking Israelis who visit the Scribner Book Store.

Miss McDaniels, one of my high-school teachers, made Latin an adventure, and I regret not having thanked her. Knowing Latin has contributed to my reading pleasure. Then there was college.

I can't recall whether it was Sidney Hook, Edwin Berry Burgum, or William Troy who pointed out that a college education was merely a skeleton of knowledge upon which we would have to build if we truly wanted to feel the full measure of life. Since I still love each of those instructors of mine at Washington Square College, I am willing to believe that each one said it.

William Troy—blond, lean, and serious—lectured on the contemporary novel. At the time they were just lectures, and I dutifully took notes. Years later and many times since, I have referred to these notes on Joyce, Proust, Mann, Virginia Woolf, D. H. Lawrence, and André Malraux. That Troy would be the force propelling me to a life of dedicated reading, I did not realize then.

In a sense, Troy and I met again in 1968 as I was snooping about in the essay section of Scribner's. I came upon a book entitled, *William Troy: Selected Essays*, published by Rutgers University Press. It was sad to learn that Troy was dead, and frustrating to realize that the posthumous recognition of his work as a brilliant literary critic came too late for him to enjoy; but Troy's intelligence made its mark on those of us who were obviously ready for him. Stanley Edgar Hyman was correct when he wrote, "Those who sat in his classes and

Celia Summer

attended his lectures, unanimously describe William Troy as the greatest of lecturers in literature."

In 1940, the job market for teachers was not much better than it is today. I had majored in English and was fully prepared to teach, but there were few teaching jobs and many of us were forced to take whatever we could find.

I applied for work in the book department of Abraham & Straus in Brooklyn. The book department was a handsome place, almost separate from the rest of the store; like Scribner's, it had a high arched ceiling and was a pleasant place to browse. I was given a book test. The applicant had to match fifty titles with authors. When I looked at the list, I chuckled; they were all taken from the inside jacket of the Modern Library books. We had used Modern Library throughout college.

I got the job and stayed until I was asked to come home to help my father in our family business.

The singular memory from my days at Abraham & Straus is the letter I sent to the *Saturday Review of Literature,* which was printed in a subsequent issue.

> Dear Sir:
> At one time, not so long ago, I worked in a rather large book shop. From time to time, situations would arise which seemed almost too precious to forego recording. One of them follows:
> "Oh, miss," a squeaky voice demanded, "I

would like to see some books in blue and white, rather small."

"Does the author matter, madam?" I asked.

"Oh, no," she retorted, "I don't care what kind they are or who wrote them. I just want them to fit in with the colors of my bedroom."

Screwing up my lips to keep some indelicate aspersions from escaping, I led the lady to a stack of small blue leather-bound English classics. Then, silently apologizing to Thackeray, Fielding, and George Eliot, I asked her if they would do. She examined one of the books as one appraises a piece of furniture.

"These won't do," she said quite annoyed, "they are only blue, and I don't care for the gilt edges. They wouldn't fit in at all. Aren't there any others in blue and white?"

"No," I replied, "books aren't usually published to conform with the colors of rooms."

She glared at me. "Insolent," she snapped, as she turned vehemently, and marched out.

Celia Summer
Brooklyn, N.Y. 1940

After my father's death, I was made an equal partner in the family business; but I found myself to be the inheritor of every job, menial or otherwise, which my dear brother Sam would not condescend to do. I attribute his attitude to a lack of regard for women which was so profound then that, though we were *equal* partners, he

Celia Summer

was drawing more salary than I—an injustice I find painful to remember. I am now convinced he was a "male chauvinist pig," but I was incapable, at the time, of arriving at such a clear, graphic definition. Of course, habitual attitudes are not easily shed.

Our family was male-dominated, and we women were, without question, the second sex. The trucking and warehouse business required much physical strength in those days, and women didn't seem to fit in too well. It is no tribute to me that I took so long to assert myself. In my simple way, I was submissive. I had not really chosen to be in the business. I had inherited a part of it because my father probably saw no other way to protect his unmarried daughter.

And so my job consisted of bookkeeping, typing, making out the payroll, making bank deposits, paying all the bills, and making social calls on people, particularly at the army installations in and around New York City—people who could help increase our business.

We were then doing domestic and export crating for army personnel under the direction of the transportation officers of Fort Jay and Fort Hamilton.

The years in my father's business served me well in spite of the difficulties I mentioned. I became a little tougher, less fearful, and more capable of facing reality. It is pleasant to recall meeting a challenge, which I believe I handled many times, with a maturity that had nothing to do with being male or female.

For instance, in the moving and trucking business, the law requires licenses for traveling from state to state or even within the same state. My father did not have these licenses, and it was decided by the "superior" partner, my brother, that we would apply to the Public Service Commission for the privilege of driving our trucks through Nassau and Suffolk counties in Long Island.

When a date was set for the hearing, my brother announced that I should go alone. His decision was based, he claimed, on the fact that I was better educated than he, therefore I would prove to be more articulate, more able to convince "them" that we deserved to be granted the license. At the time, I was furious, but I now know he was right. In retrospect, it is clear that though he raved and ranted within the confines of our office and warehouse, going out into the world with his vitriolic temper would have been foolhardy. He was simply not at ease outside the trucking business.

I remember deciding that for this occasion, I would shine, and I resorted to the devices women have used for centuries. I primped, I fussed, I wore my best suit and a hat to match. I was going to prove myself to me, to him, to all. I realized to some extent then, but more fully later on, that it was unusual for a woman to appear at such a hearing. Fighting for a trucking license was definitely a man's business.

I was the only woman in the little courtroom. Those present were a male court stenographer, a male judge, and about twelve over-sized men who seemed to be some kind of a jury. I must confess I was frightened. I leaned over to the stenographer, and meekly inquired as to the status of the big twelve. I learned they were people in competitive businesses, and they were there to protest my application. In typically feminine fashion, I was totally appalled and shocked that these characters could possibly consider me a threat (which, in reality, I was).

The judge appeared. We stood as he entered the chamber. He examined my papers and asked a few questions to which I demurely responded. With a sudden motion, he removed his glasses and asked, "Young lady, how long has your family been in this business in Brooklyn?"

"My father started it in 1905 with four large horses and a wagon," I answered.

"Well," he said benignly, with a twinkle in his eye, "there is no problem. According to the law, you are entitled to what we call 'Grandfather Rights,' which means you have been in business long enough to have earned this privilege."

I gathered my papers together, smoothed my clothes, and stalked out of the room, my very first victory secured. But though I was very proud to have been granted the license, and proud to be a woman, I was not to know real pride and freedom until I finally left the family business.

I wanted to know what it would be like to work out there in the world again without being bullied and feeling fearful. It turned out to be absolutely great! Ultimately, I guess I am a slow learner, and it took me a long time to find my own identity, but it certainly was the most worthwhile goal.

After an extended, forced vacation because of two stints in the operating room, I called an old friend,

With A Book in My Hand

Blanche Cirker, who had worked closely with me at the Abraham & Straus book shop. (She and her husband are now the publishers of Dover Books.) Without hesitation, she suggested I go directly to Scribner's to apply for a job. "Books are your great love, and selling them is what you do best, you know," she said.

I lost no time acting on Blanche's suggestion and applied for a job at the Scribner Book Store in September 1965. I had the advantage of having had previous experience and had also kept up with things going on in the book world. The time was right, too. It was before Christmas, a time for hiring, and so they asked me to start on October 15th. That's how it all began.

After I began to work at Scribner's and observe my coworkers and the general environment I sort of missed the "hardy" characters in the trucking world and I found myself making unconscious comparisons. Suddenly I was nostalgic for some of my "tough guy" worker friends.

When I consider the lethargy of some of the men under thirty who take jobs as book-sellers, and gripe about meager salaries as they stand around computing the income of their bosses (who may have invested many years to achieve a lofty position), when I see these young men spending much of their time looking forward to their coffee breaks, watching the female employees carry heavy books without reaching out to offer a helping hand, I can't help remembering with a certain longing the days when young fellows of the same age came to work for my father in the trucking and warehousing business.

It is true our men were laborers, their formal education was limited, but their willingness to produce, to endure hardships, in short, to prove themselves, was something wonderful. There was no piano too big to carry up and down flights of stairs or to carefully hoist up several floors—even if the risks were considerable. Such a man was Archie Rowe, a young, lean, handsome West Indian who came to work for my father in 1930.

Although we were already a family of seven children, two boys, five girls, Archie became a third son to my father and a third brother to me. His warmth, his kindness, counteracted the behavior of my brothers who practiced sibling rivalry to an inordinate degree.

Archie must have decided to learn all he could from my father with whom he closely identified and whom he deeply respected.

My father, Jacob Summer, was a tall, portly man, well-dressed (by Witty Brothers), intimidating, dictatorial, but nonetheless a man to be admired; self-made, sole owner of a business, and a man who could boast of having no debts. Neither could he read nor write English.

"As long as I can sign a check and back that check up with money in the bank, I can do anything," he assured us.

This was the man Archie emulated. In the end, it

paid off. Archie started his own trucking business fifteen years later and became quite successful. He continues to be a friend and an adopted brother; but ever since Pop died, Archie and my brother Harry do not always get on well.

One day, Archie ran out of his supply of dish packs (containers used for packing dishes for transport). With his helper, Haywood, Archie drove over to my brother's place to see about borrowing some.

Unfortunately, Harry had come to resent Archie as a competitor (and probably had long resented him as an "adopted" brother), and he turned Archie down, claiming he was out of dish packs, too.

In the intimate, brotherly style to which they'd become accustomed, Archie retorted, "Harry, you're a damned liar. I need those dish packs, and I'm giving you your last chance."

"What do you mean by my 'last chance,' big mouth?" asked Harry.

"Listen," Archie retorted, "If you don't give me those dish packs, so help me God, I'm going up to the cemetery and tell Mom and Pop about your disgusting behavior toward me in business. Me, your own brother."

Harry didn't respond, and so Archie stalked out of the office and told Haywood to drive him to the Summer family plot in the Cypress Hills cemetery. There, Archie went over and sat down on the stone bench which my father had requested be placed for just such occasions.

Haywood, not daring to imagine what terrible thing had happened to his boss, meekly asked, "Mr. Rowe, do you mind if I wait for you in the car?"

Celia Summer

Archie waved him away. He just sat on the stone bench a while and then, feeling he had paid his respects to his surrogate parents, he got back into the car and directed Haywood to drive him back to my brother's warehouse.

As they entered Harry's office, Archie said to Haywood, "Tell him where we've been and what I did."

"I dunno, Mr. Summer," Haywood said, "I think Mr. Rowe's crazy. He sat on that bench up in the cemetery and said, 'I want you to talk to your first son, and tell him he is not treating me right'."

My brother—visibly shaken—said to Archie, "Did you really go up to the cemetery?"

"I did," said Archie. "You are my brother and you've got no right refusing me anything."

Brother Harry slowly walked into the warehouse and called out to old-timer Charlie White, "Hey, Charlie—give this big mouth what he wants and get him the hell out of here. This son-of-a-bitch has been up to the cemetery to report me to Pop."

With that, Charlie produced ten dish packs, and Archie left in triumph.

I genuinely believe there are few formally educated young men with whom I have worked at Scribner's who would be capable of Archie Rowe's directness and ingenuity. I still bet on the fellows of the warehouse set.

Some young fellows, who seem promising when they start their employment at Scribner's, master the art of relaxation in a relatively short time. The lunch hour gradually becomes lunch *hours*, the coffee breaks grow longer. Perhaps I am old-fashioned, but I get the

With A Book in My Hand

impression that their goal is to achieve a minimum amount of labor with a maximum amount of arrogance.

There was once a precept about the satisfaction of doing a good day's work. It must have gone the way of white gloves and polished shoes.

In the mood for reminiscing about my years at Scribner's, I know there are certain unforgettable personalities in the literary world who will remain indelibly in my mind, just as those who enriched my working days and enlarged my vision, have become deeply engraved in my heart.

There are several marvelous and irreplaceable gentlemen who people the book world, and I'm afraid they are the last of a noble breed.

A meticulously dressed, portly man with a round cherubic face, a black derby, and monocle seemed rather formidable at first; but he was a voracious reader. He would wander about the Scribner Book Store gathering books. He used the monocle from time to time as he inspected his quarry, and when both arms were fully laden, he would request that his collection be shipped home. For him, home could be New York City or Kansas. At first, there was not much communication between us,

Celia Summer

and I respected his distance. After a year or so he thawed a little, and I soon began to receive friendly notes with a touch of humor, requesting some new book or other that struck his fancy. During the second year, I read in the newspapers that he was nearly banished from Fisher's Island for throwing a lobster party at a joint where only ship workers congregated; that's when I truly began to admire him.

As our friendship grew, he told me his favorite jokes, including a sprinkling of Jewish jokes which he realized I understood well. He became more flexible, even a little mischievous. A time came when he even permitted me to suggest new reading material. Then I knew we were really fast friends.

On a Saturday morning in the fall of 1972, he came to fetch a few new books. With tears in his eyes, he told me that he had cancer and was on his way to the hospital for an operation. I walked him out of the store, hailed a taxi, and kissed him goodbye. Then I turned away and wept.

This man was William Lindsay White, the publisher of *The Emporia Gazette* of Kansas, writer and roving reporter, and author of *Journey For Margaret*, which was a best-seller in the 1940s.

When I returned from vacation at the end of June 1973, I received a message that Mr. White had called me from a hospital in Emporia. I was eager to talk with him and phoned at once. I opened the conversation with a light touch, asking if he had heard any good jokes lately. His voice was fragile, but he retorted, "This hospital doesn't seem to be a place for jokes. I called you among other things because there's a book out in London on Evelyn Waugh."

I knew the one he meant, but it was not ready for publication in America, and I assured him (knowing in my heart there wasn't much time left for him) that if I got my hands on it he would have it pronto. After a slight pause, he said, "I love you."

"Same here," I answered softly. There was a knot in my throat.

"I might see you in a while," he said.

"Great," I said, "and in the meantime I'll try to dig up some awful jokes for you."

On July 27, 1973, *The New York Times* ran a lengthy obituary on my friend. I wrote to Mrs. White:

> It is with much sadness that I acknowledge the obituary of Mr. White in *The New York Times*. I will miss him—that derby, that monocle, that delightful sense of humor, the dignity with which he carried himself, and, most of all, I am happy I was able to speak with him recently over the phone. He was, I feel, the last of a certain breed of gentlemen. I am honored to have known him.

Soon after, Mrs. White sent me a note and clippings of the tributes to Mr. White which appeared in *The Emporia Gazette*. Someone said he looked like Winston Churchill, and that was true. Perhaps that was what appealed to me at first, but it was also the twinkling eyes, the robust humor, and his zest for life and books. I will always cherish her words:

Dear Miss Summer,
 Bill loved your call—your letters and you—me too.
                              Kathrine White

Another special visitor to Scribner's is Sir John Wheeler-Bennett, an eminent historian and authority on German history, who has been coming to the United States each year to lecture at New York University and the University of Arizona. Sir John is typically British—tall, lean, dignified with his cane; he reads voraciously and professes to enjoy the cartoon, *Peanuts.* I think he resembles the movie actor Roger Livesey, and he oozes an effortless charm. Sir John is surely one of the last of the Renaissance men.

I asked Dr. A. L. Rowse, of All Souls, Oxford, who was in the store one winter afternoon, if he knew Sir John Wheeler-Bennett, and proceeded to tell him how much some of us at Scribner's admired Sir John. With tongue-in-cheek shock, and superb mock indignation, he said to me, "How can you possibly like him more than me? I am younger and handsomer!"

At that point, I remarked, "Were you knighted as well?"

He replied that people did not think much of knighthood nowadays. So-called "honors" suffered from inflation, like everything else. Honors are a devalued

With A Book in My Hand

currency. He felt that his friend T. S. Eliot, for example, would probably not have accepted a knighthood. Nor would Gilbert Murray, the classical scholar, G. M. Trevelyan, the historian, George Bernard Shaw, or H. G. Wells.

According to Dr. Rowse, in recent years J. B. Priestley and Charles Morgan each turned down knighthood. Rudyard Kipling and A. E. Housman, poet and classical scholar, turned down the Order of Merit—Housman because it had been conferred on John Galsworthy whom he considered second rate.

Dr. Rowse feels that neither a decent sense of values nor adequare standards exist today. And he feels deeply and seriously about this.

Dr. Rowse is self-confident, robust, charming, and utterly delightful. We have shared some joyous moments over coffee and muffins at a nearby coffee shop where this dear Shakespearean authority told me about himself. Dr. Rowse considers himself a Cornishman, not an Englishman, and he told me that most Cornishmen of that name spell Rowse with a "w." He told me of an English murderer (Arthur A. Rouse) who was proven guilty, condemned to death, and hanged. After the execution, an Oxford don entered a room filled with several men and greeted them by saying, "Hi! They've hanged the wrong Rowse."

The chairwoman of a luncheon club in England's North Country asked her husband to write a thank-you speech to be delivered when A. L. Rowse, the guest of honor, finished his talk.

Celia Summer

When she began to speak, she noticed that her husband had written it in honor of Sir Stanley Rouse, chairman of the National Football Association—the only Rouse he had probably ever heard of. Sir Stanley was much more widely known among football fans and the general public in England. But the other side of the joke was that Dr. A. L. Rowse was equally surprised. He in turn had never heard of the national football figure, Sir Stanley Rouse. In any case, I suppose it is ironic that the football figure was knighted and not our authority on Elizabethan England.

Perhaps Dr. Rowse would be pleased if, in the future they say of him—as Hilaire Belloc wrote of himself:

> When I am dead
> I hope it will be said
> That—though his sins were scarlet—
> Yet his books were read.

As a bookseller, I *know* Dr. Rowse's books are read widely in this country.

From him I learned that scholars chosen to write royal biographies are usually knighted. In the Middle Ages or the Elizabethan Age, it meant something. But Dr. Rowse feels that it all has very little meaning today. As far as he is concerned, official biographies of royal personages have produced some of the most unreadable rubbish—stuffed with cotton wool, thick with sycophancy and humbug.

Consider, he suggested, Sir Theodore Martin's five volumes on Queen Victoria's sainted Prince Consort; or

With A Book in My Hand

Sidney Lee's two volumes on Edward VII—almost as fat as that old gourmand himself. Actually, Edward VII was the complete philistine—interested only in women and horses. However, he had enough sense of the good to say to Sidney Lee on meeting him "Stick to Shakespeare, Mr. Lee! There's money in it!"

And there was. Sidney Lee wrote the best-selling biography of Shakespeare for his time, as Dr. Rowse has for ours. Sidney Lee's official biography of Edward VII is, to use T.S. Eliot's phrase, "dead as a dead duck."

So far, Dr. Rowse has not written anything official, let alone a dead-as-a-duck biography. Instead he has written about the real Elizabethan Age and its figures—Sir Walter Raleigh, Sir Richard Grenville, Shakespeare, Christopher Marlowe, and Shakespeare's patron, Southampton, one of the founders of Virginia. Dr. Rowse finds inspiration in Shakespeare's age—when England, youthful and vigorous, first achieved greatness. He used to be asked, when Elizabeth II became queen, if there was any chance of this becoming a second Elizabethan Age for Britain.

"Not on your life!" was the answer. "Nothing can be expected from a society that sets its pace by the slackest, where nobody wants to do any work, that discourages initiative and ruins incentive—quite unlike Drake and Raleigh, Marlow and Shakespeare—that has no standards, hates what is first rate and envies achievement; a second-rate country, bent on becoming a third-rate one. Perhaps the one good thing is that it provides me the right setting and condition of mind for an historian; for the past of

Celia Summer

Britain is a great deal more interesting than its future is likely to be." Dr. Rowse finds more zest and enterprise, more incentive, more of the Elizabethan spirit in America. In the interval of writing books and lecturing in the United States—he has spoken at some two hundred universities, colleges, and schools—we are fortunate to have him come to our book store for a chat or to buy something unexpected: the stories of Mark Twain or the short stories of Flannery O'Connor, the modern American author of whom he has the highest admiration.

Since Dr. Rowse had reacted so strongly against the Order of Merit, I found it almost imperative to discuss the subject with Sir John Wheeler-Bennett; after all, I do have great respect for his opinions. I must naively confess that not until very recently did I discover that Sir John, an historian, was also special assistant to the director general of Information Services on International Affairs for Great Britain, a visiting professor at a number of American universities, a lecturer in international law, head of the New York Office of British Political Warfare Mission in the United States from 1942 until 1944, attached to the British prosecuting team at the War Criminal Trial in Nuremberg in 1946, British editor-in-chief of captured German Foreign Ministry Archives, and a lecturer in international politics at New College, Oxford. He has written innumerable books on Germany and on the life and reign of King George VI.

In Sir John's opinion, the Order of Merit is one of the most distinguished honors which anyone in the field of politics, science, or literature can possibly receive. It is

With A Book in My Hand

one of the few orders which is a direct and unfettered gift of the Sovereign and is bestowed through her own initiative. It therefore creates a unique and much valued link between the Queen and the recipient.

These two are men of considerable accomplishment. I found them to be most delightful, and I am sorry to say that I cannot find many like them.

I suppose I love these men because they seem larger than life to me. In our business, we meet so many people, but just a few make an indelible impression—I suppose that's what I mean by "larger than life." In fact, as I consider it, what stays with me as I think of them is their wit, their capacity to achieve, and still retain a kind of humor which I consider indispensable to survival in this not-so-sensible world.

When I was in charge of the reference books in 1968, part of my daily routine was to sell dictionaries, which I enjoyed since I love dictionaries of all descriptions. At the same time (and in quiet moments) I was rereading Bemelmans' *Madeline* series, and all the Babars, and *Winnie-the-Pooh*, and I took on *Charlotte's Web* and *Stuart Little*. I was sorry I had waited so long to enjoy such reading pleasures, and I was happy to discover that Stuart, the little mouse, recommended Webster's Col-

Celia Summer

legiate Dictionary to his class of students. It sounded sensible to me.

Only a few days after devouring the E. B. White books, an elderly, gray-haired man approached me and gently asked if I would send two copies of the Collegiate dictionary to his home in Maine. I guess my ESP must have been working rather well because without hesitation I declared, "You must be E. B. White!"

"Yes, I am," he responded quietly.

I took him by the hand and proudly led him to our juvenile department and introduced him to my fellow workers.

Mr. White was not a frequent visitor to the store, but in December of 1972, Diane Berkeley of the children's book section rushed over to me as I came back from lunch to spill her story. She said an elderly gent had come into the store requesting assistance in choosing some books for his grandchildren. She thought of recommending *Stuart Little* or *Charlotte's Web*, but somewhere inside herself, she felt the customer wouldn't know what on earth she was talking about, and so she showed him, instead, the newer books of the year. As she wrapped his purchases, he asked her to charge them.

"To whom shall I charge these, sir?" Diane asked.

"To E. B. White," he replied, "of North Brooklin, Maine."

Soon after, I received an order of books with a note:

Dear Miss Summer,

I missed seeing you when I was in the store one

With A Book in My Hand

day last week, but a very pleasant young lady took care of my needs.

Sincerely,
E. B. White

Mr. White and I met again when he was in New York to be near his wife who was hospitalized in the city. There was a forlorn look about him. Something made me bring up the subject of a wonderful letter he had written to the A.S.P.C.A. (It is reprinted in his book *The Second Tree from the Corner*.) It seems that the Society had accused him of harboring an unlicensed dog. Minnie, the dachshund, *was* in fact licensed in the state of Maine. I just had to tell Mr. White how much I'd enjoyed that letter. He looked at me wistfully, "I just wish Minnie could be with me now."

When *The Trumpet of the Swan* was published in the summer of 1970, I received a copy of the book from North Brooklin inscribed as follows:

For Celia Summer
with a loud Ko-Hoh
from E. B. White

A long time ago, Mr. White wrote a priceless essay on dog training. I could never approach his style or wit, but I would love to tell him how it was for me, and I think this is as good a time as any. It took place in my pre-Scribner days.

Celia Summer

Since our house adjoined our warehouse in Brooklyn, we had considerable property to watch over and I realized one day that it would be a great comfort for me to have a watchdog and helper. A German shepherd seemed most likely. Also, I loved the breed.

From the moment I walked into the kennel, I fell captive to a seven-week-old puppy. It has been attested to by other dog owners that puppies frequently make the decision: the puppy fussed over me and I surrendered. I had no alternative, I paid the price and left with my little bundle, thinking her name would be Julia.

I placed her gently and cautiously in a carton on the seat next to mine in the car, because I'd been warned about car-sickness in puppies on their first excursion. By the time we reached home, she had fulfilled my awful expectations and had made quite a mess.

In her first weeks with me, the loss and damage were pervasive: scratched upholstery, gnawed shoes and bedslippers, chewed rugs, and a mysterious disappearance of kitchen utensils and toys, but I believed all the destruction was absolutely necessary for the growth and development of a pet's teeth, and I had been told she would stop after she was one year old. I calculated that the repairs cost me about two hundred and fifty dollars—a conservative estimate.

A good—and forthright—friend suggested that I quickly enroll Julia in a canine-training school. I was warned that unless Julia was disciplined properly, she would grow up big, strong, and totally uncontrollable. Thus I joined the German Shepherd Club of Long

With A Book in My Hand

Island, determined to make the twenty-mile drive each week. By this time, her car-sickness was a thing of the past and was replaced by a Pavlovian compulsion which induced Julia to withdraw her head from the open car window, and to shove her snout into my face for a few sloppy smooches. God's hand surely guided us through the heavy traffic. Julia's wet kisses still remind me of *My Eyes Have a Cold Nose*, a wonderful book written by Hector de Chevigny who was blind.

On the first visit, Julia and I were eyed up and down by every human and canine member of the club. The snooty atmosphere was enough to convince me we'd never make it, for Julia was a poor specimen of her breed, and although she could surely be trained for obedience, her chances for competition were nil. I cherished her floppy ears, but her rear end was too high. This dog club was only interested in perfection, I soon discovered, so we quit. Julia must have known instantly I was her Jewish mother.

She began to reform—adopting the ways of the workers in the warehouse. If they had a coffee break in the morning, she had a coffee break. If they drank beer, she drank beer. If I couldn't find her, chances were she was riding up and down the freight elevator with the men, acting busy and useful. In the cold weather, you would be sure to find her within the glow of the potbellied stove that the men maintained for themselves. Occasionally, she got bored with the fellows and decided to visit me. To do this, she had to climb a spiral staircase,

Celia Summer

at which she had become skillful, and then scratch on my house door. (This was a special connection between warehouse and home.) She would carefully take everything in, then drape herself limply on the best chair near a window to watch for possible enemies.

One day my brother had a huge steak thawing near the kitchen sink, and I know he was really looking forward to eating it. Julia had meandered into the house, led by the delicious aroma, but I was too busy to notice. Suddenly, I heard terrible sounds, both animal and human. My brother's voice cried out, "I'll kill her, if I get my hands on her!"

I had to see what had happened. "What did she do?" I asked meekly, sensing danger.

"What did she do?" he bellowed, "nothing much—that beast just stole and devoured my steak and I'm going to kill her!"

"Over my dead body!" I yelled back as I flew out of the house, down the spiral staircase into the warehouse to protect Julia. We stayed away until Sam had calmed down. And I felt, rather righteously, that he was the guilty party, not the dog. No intelligent human being leaves meat within the reach of a big, healthy dog.

In time, the pressures of the business were such that I decided to part with dear Julia. To appease my conscience, I came up with the idea that it would indeed be a decent gesture to offer her to the Seeing-Eye of Morristown, New Jersey, which was then the foremost dog-guide center on the East Coast. There, she could be

With A Book in My Hand

trained to help the blind, I told myself. We were well received. Julia was in excellent health and ripe for such work.

After a difficult parting, I assumed that time would heal the wound. Time turned out to be a huge faker. I began to miss the leash in my hand wherever I walked, the cold wet nose near my face when I sat, the dirty paws on the clean floors, the seventy pounds of beast that occasionally curled up next to me as if it were no more than a puppy. After two weeks of separation, I lost all resolve, telephoned the Seeing-Eye, and meekly told them of my misgivings. I was reassuringly informed that I was not the first donor who displayed such symptoms, and that they would be happy to return her to me, particularly since they had not begun to train her, nor had she been spayed. Julia and I were reunited with their blessings. Thereafter we shared many happy experiences.

I did not plan to have Julia mated early, but she made her own decision on this point. One day, she took to her bed, refusing to budge except for necessities. She assumed a mournful appearance—a look of doom. Eventually, I wooed her into the car to consult with the veterinarian. He pointed out that she was going through a false pregnancy, and that I could look forward to many more....

When she was five years old, Julia, accidentally caused the most serious injury I've ever sustained. I was about to take her for her usual noontime walk. With leash in hand, I leaned on a high work table in our warehouse. The sight of the leash brought excitement, and she made

Celia Summer

an attempt to leap to the table. My face was in the way. I felt a tremendous blow on my mouth, something akin to a fall of a sledge hammer. I felt no pain, though, only numbness and a swift flow of blood from my mouth. My two front teeth felt loose. Somehow, with a will born of shock, I got into my car and managed to drive five city blocks to my dentist's office.

Immediately, he applied an antiseptic to my entire mouth, x-rayed my teeth, and suggested I go home to get some rest. At midnight, the agonizing pain began. Our family doctor rushed over. He administered morphine and I passed out. At 4 A.M. other members of my family began to arrive. They were called by a sister who was living with me then. At 7 A.M. my blood pressure had dropped to an amazing low, and a decision was made to have x-rays of my skull taken to check for possible concussion.

By the time I returned home, in twenty-degree weather, I had a high fever plus a yellow and purple face. Then emerged the largest lip I had ever seen. It was so abominable to look at, that I would not allow visitors to see anything but half my face. The rest was covered with a small towel.

For the next ten days, a doctor and a dentist visited me simultaneously. It was almost impossible to determine where the need for one ended and the need for the other began.

Strong sedatives, taken every four hours, day and night, produced many strange reactions, including technicolor dreams and arms and legs jerking involuntarily.

With A Book in My Hand

Once my hand jumped up by its own volition, and hit my face in the vulnerable area. I had had it. I began to cry with such self-pity that I vowed I'd rather suffer pain than endure these strange manifestations. I have been informed since—that these symptoms occur in people who are addicted to narcotics. Even when I began to be ambulatory, I slouched around like a robot with a very glassy stare.

As for Julia, well, she managed to sneak forlornly into my bedroom and her sad-sack expression dissolved my resolution to excommunicate her. I took her back into the fold and also looked to her for comfort and solace—she was, in truth, a wise dog, though of an exuberant nature.

Julia would indeed have loved Mr. White's goose—the one on the Op-Ed page of *The New York Times* (August 15, 1973). It seems that the *Times* asked Mr. White for the reactions of his barnyard to the Watergate affair. And so, Mr. White had a consultation with his arrogant goose who felt, indeed, that G. Gordon Liddy was a bungler of immense promise, that Nixon should resign in favor of Liddy, that Strachan was "tainted with honesty—a complete misfit." Goose also felt that Senator Sam Ervin was out of step with the country's corruption, dirty tricks, payola, kickbacks, etcetera.

When Mr. White asked Goose for suggestions for legislation to prevent the events of Watergate, Goose recommended that the dirty tricks department be elevated to full cabinet status.

I have no right to go on with this, and would suggest

Celia Summer

that readers take a look at this marvelous comment. I immediately wrote to Mr. White to express my appreciation. This was his reply:

October 3, 1973

Dear Miss Summer:

What a pleasure to get your letter! I wrote that Watergate piece at the tag end of a long illness that sent me finally into the hospital. Just before entering, I mailed the piece to the *Times*. Then I had qualms about it, and the day I came out of the hospital I phoned Herb Mitgang at the *Times* and asked him to kill the piece. He chuckled gleefully and informed me that it had appeared in the paper that morning, complete with a silhouette of me and the goose.

Glad you like it. Liddy is still my man for President, with Segretti heading up the F.B.I.

Sincerely,
E.B. White

Without reservation, I believe E.B. White is one of the finest essayists of our time. His combination of integrity, perception and humor, plus his complete lack of affectation touch me, and give me hope that if there were only more people like E.B. White, we might find the world a better place to live in.

With A Book in My Hand

An attractive young man asked me if I had the book, *Judenrat*, by Isaiah Trunk on hand. I produced it immediately. He then asked for *Children of Pride* which was on the same counter. "Ah, this is the quickest response I've had in this city. What luck! I must confess—I am the author of *Children of Pride*," he exclaimed.

As has become my custom, I immediately asked if he would do a bit of autographing, and Robert Manson Myers seemed happy to comply. We talked. He had come to New York to accept the National Book Award. His book, *Children of Pride*, and *Judenrat* were sharing the award for history that year. The split vote seemed to me to disturb him. I knew his book had done very well through Christmas and right up to the present in spite of the twenty-dollar price tag. It had received high praise from some of the most prestigious periodicals and critics. I believe Mr. Myers had even considered rejecting the award, as if sharing it was somehow demeaning.

Since he asked for my opinion, and since I said what he probably wanted me to say, it made for a happy moment all around.

"It seems to me that you ought to forget the split vote completely. I think you should be grateful for the honor—accept and acknowledge your joy in the entire experience. At least, this is what I would do," I said.

He stood there almost speechless, and then with

Celia Summer

much pleasure, he said, "I sensed you had heart, but you've mind as well. You have made my day."

Several days later, I received the following letter:

Dear Miss Summer,

My visit to Scribner's was so pleasant, and your kindly interest in me was so opportune and generous, that I send you this line to tell you that I appreciate your warmth, enthusiasm, and sympathy at a time when all three were most welcome! You are the ideal person to live in the world of books and to represent them to others, and I wish there were more like you to make them attractive and readily available to all. I shall be in New York again on 9 May to receive an award for *Children of Pride*, and I hope I shall be able to come into Scribner's and enjoy your friendly reception once more. With all good wishes,

Yours sincerely,
Robert Manson Myers

On April 30, 1973, *Publishers Weekly* gave this report on the National Book Awards:

Mr. Myers, whose *Children of Pride* (Yale University Press) shared the History prize with Isaiah Trunk's *Judenrat* (Macmillan), gave off thrilling emanations from the start. Asked whether he objected to sharing his prize, he responded, "I shall have something to say about that this evening," with such an air of menacing hauteur that reporters commenced upon the spot to sharpen their pencils for Tully Hall. As it turned out, however, Mr. Myers did not create the sort of sensation that had been anticipated—though rumors persisted that he had planned to denounce the idea of sharing awards in his acceptance speech, and had only been prevailed upon to reject this approach at the last moment.

Even his prepared speech, however, was not lacking in effect. Sneering at the (unnamed) publishers who had rejected his book, quoting amiably from a review that described it as "an American *War and Peace*," and at length from a "beautiful" fan letter that said, "I know that this monumental work will stand as a permanent tribute to your name," he delivered a speech of such tingling immodesty that people all over the hall were stifling incredulous guffaws.

Many years ago, I was deeply impressed by the book *A Many Splendored Thing* by Han Suyin, and I continued to read each Han Suyin book as it was published. This charming Eurasian doctor seemed to handle her deep private and political conflicts with remarkable courage. I

Celia Summer

thoroughly enjoyed her autobiography in the form of three novels, *The Crippled Tree*, *A Mortal Flower*, and *Birdless Summer*.

It was no wonder then, that as a book-seller, I was thrilled to have been invited to a cocktail party (at 6:30 on a cold Tuesday night in October 1972) given by Little, Brown and Company for Han Suyin to celebrate the publication of her book, *The Morning Deluge*—the story of the Chinese revolution.

The event was memorable for me. Dan Schloeske, a co-worker, and I found our way to an apartment by the East River where the author stayed when she visited New York. Since most of the faces there were unfamiliar, we took our drinks and sat down quietly in the corner of the room. Then I saw Han Suyin—high cheekbones, easy smile, looking trim and lovely. We introduced ourselves as representatives of the Scribner Book Store. She was very cordial but was soon drawn away by two young men who wanted to discuss the pandas given to the United States after President Nixon's visit to China.

After a reasonable time, Dan and I decided to leave and Han Suyin, although busy with others, came over to say goodbye. I could not resist inviting her to our book store to do some autographing. It was just before Christmas, and I knew our customers would be delighted to have the chance to buy inscribed books for Christmas gifts.

Two days later I received a telephone call from the publicity department of Little, Brown announcing that Han Suyin would pay us a visit at 3 P.M.

With A Book in My Hand

She arrived promptly. As she walked toward me in a smartly tailored suit, I noticed that the buttons on her cerise double-breasted jacket were hanging loosely. After a cordial greeting, she said briskly, "I will sign about a dozen books—no more."

"Dr. Han Suyin, do you know that all the buttons on your coat are loose?" I asked quickly.

"Yes," she responded, "but I hate sewing."

"In that case," I replied, "if you sign, I will sew."

She looked at me quizzically, but did not argue. We retreated to a desk at the rear of the store where I always kept a small sewing kit.

"Do you wish," she asked, "my signature in English or Chinese?"

"Do whatever pleases you," I replied as I began to reinforce all the buttons. She autographed in both languages. In my copy, she wrote bilingually:

> To Celia Summer
> With Happy Affection

We talked a bit, and I blurted out how *Man's Fate* by André Malraux had had such a profound effect upon me. She understood.

Later in December, I received the following letter from her from Switzerland:

> Dear Celia Summer,
>   This is only a short note from someone recovering from a bad bout of intestinal flu (that's me). You should have seen me, in bed, incapable of

Celia Summer

getting up for about three weeks! I have often thought of wonderful you, sewing on my buttons for me, and thought that if you were around, you would have got me into shape with some famous recipe for flu, and got me back to work in no time.

I shall be back in America at the end of January, and be certain that one of the first people I shall come to see will be you. Meanwhile, please accept my very good wishes for Christmas and the New Year 1973. God bless you.

Sincerely,
Han Suyin

I wrote back saying, yes, I had a remedy for the flu—tender loving care plus chicken soup with rice.

As promised, she came back to New York and one fine Saturday morning in February, we sat sat face to face over coffee and blueberry muffins in a luncheonette on 49th street. As I looked at her, I asked myself, "Is this the woman who gave up a brilliant career in medicine for writing? Is this the delicate woman whose first husband, a Nationalist general in Chiang-Kai-Shek's army, beat her up at the slightest provocation, and most often, with no reason except the projections of his own distorted mind?"

Then I asked her, "Are you now married again?"

She replied, "Yes, for seventeen years—did you not see that black man at the cocktail party?"

"I saw a tall, handsome Indian, but I did not know who he was," I replied.

"You have grace," she commented.

Then we talked. It was such a joy to communicate

With A Book in My Hand

with someone who knew exactly what I felt even before I finished a sentence.

I now feel that for Han Suyin, writing was as natural as breathing. She had to cry out in words just as an American Indian poet did when he wrote: "We have cried so long, Our cry has become song."

As a Eurasian, she belonged to two worlds—both in a sense rejecting her. Her mother considered this daughter ugly, but Han Suyin found it wasn't so when the boys trailed after her during her growing-up years.

She was not only recalcitrant, but also brilliant in her perceptions, in her feelings; she had a sense of urgency, so admirable in people of courage, to understand the rush of events surrounding her life. I doubt that I have ever met a person more courageous or honest in my entire life.

She thought, she questioned, she defied the rules—and most of all—she has displayed a compassion for mankind and a feeling for justice which I find almost impossible to describe.

In the last seven years, she has toured the world lecturing to various audiences—students and older people—explaining the new China and answering questions wherever they were raised. Now, Han Suyin hardly ever receives the opposition that beset her when she first began these lectures. This was the woman I sat with, drinking coffee, and I felt wonderful and important.

I shall digress a bit here, but I thought I'd mention that I gave a signed copy of *The Morning Deluge* to Pearl S. Buck's secretary when she came at Christmastime to purchase the book for her boss, and shortly after I received the following note:

Celia Summer

Dear Ms. Summer:

   Miss Buck is delighted with the autographed Han Suyin book, and has asked me to thank you for your thoughtfulness. She is resting comfortably, and the doctors are pleased with her progress, but of course, her activities and personal correspondence will be curtailed for some time. Reading is one of her pleasures during this period of recuperation.

   Sincerely,
   Mrs. Beverly Drake
   Secretary to Pearl S. Buck

Miss Buck died not long after I received this letter.

But to get back, Han Suyin and I met briefly in September 1973, and over our teacups, it occurred to us that all the literary magazines and other relevant material that I receive would serve well where people were hungry for them. Some time later while Dr. Suyin was recuperating from a serious attack of hepatitis in Switzerland, I began to mail these magazines to her. This was her response:

Dear Celia,
   Thank you so much for the most magnificent gift of books and magazines, etc., most of which I have now perused and sent off to China, where authors and writers are hungry for such things. I am thus making double use of it, which I am sure pleases you. I am also very very happy that you

have been so encouraged to write; it is not an art, just a mode of expression, which should come like breathing; and I look forward to seeing you proudly autograph your book at Scribner's; I shall come myself to get a copy autographed.

My health is better and I am working again on the second volume of Mao, which is much more difficult than the first. The first is slowly asserting itself and I hear that in some universities it is being used for teaching material, which is all to the good. Unfortunately public opinion in America is so conditioned as to shrink from anything that appears "difficult"; and as to wanting "objectivity" they only mean that one must pick nits off a man. Nit picking may be pleasant, but in a way it is mean, and I do not see how, when one is confronted with such a great work as changing one quarter of humanity in such a short time, one can be so silly as to ask for "nits"; however, I do have some sizable nits to pick in the second volume, so perhaps the American public by then will be more accustomed to China being after all not a bad thing, and to speaking about Mao in disparaging terms but in a more sane and balanced way.

With all very good wishes and love to you.

Suyin

I suppose I was so happy to put my collected periodicals to use for others to enjoy, that I probably sent a more than ample amount. I included a book called *The*

Celia Summer

Arab Mind by Patai, which was published by Charles Scribner's Sons, and which I felt was absolutely brilliant. As a matter of fact, many of the Arab delegates to the United Nations bought the book in quantity. I imagine they wanted to know what an Israeli scholar came up with in the way of an anthropological study. I wanted my friend to be familiar with it since she was apt to come into contact with political problems in the Middle East. I thought she would find the book useful.

Her response came in the form of a Christmas letter which I must include now:

Dearest Celia,

You are a very wonderful and thoughtful friend! It was lovely to get more parcels, and also *The Arab Mind*, which I have not yet begun. But please don't overburden yourself with caring for me and my book-hungry friends! You must concentrate on writing your own book now.

I thought instead of sending you a Christmas card (I *never* send them anyway) I would write you a "nice hand" letter. It is for me increasingly difficult to write by hand. The typewriter spoils one completely. But I do sometimes, on special occasions and for special people, seize my fountain-pen, fill it with ink, and feel I've gone back in time, which is sweet-bitter, to the time when I filled notebooks with silly poems....

I may be coming back to New York in mid-

With A Book in My Hand

March, and do hope to see you then. As usual I shall just escape to get to Scribner's, look around, and you will come out of a door, arms full of books.

With much affection, and very good wishes for the New Year (and Christmas, though I personally dislike Christmas).

December 7, 1973

Love,
Suyin

It was the fall of 1976, my book was almost finished, and Han Suyin was in New York to celebrate the publication of her second volume, *Wind in the Tower*, which brings her history of the Chinese revolution up to date—1949 to 1975. Always encouraging, she wrote in my copy of her book,

> To dearest Celia—
> Looking forward to the great success of
> "With A Book in My Hand"
> from someone whose life is books and authors
> and with love—

We chatted in the store. "You seem to have a very recent photo of yourself on the jacket of the book," I remarked, smiling.

"It would be dishonest if I had used an early picture of myself. I believe readers should see me as I am today,"

Celia Summer

she replied with honesty. I thought of all the authors who use photos of themselves as they were ten or twenty years ago.

Han Suyin was to be on David Susskind's program that night. I had never seen her on television. Wanting to sleep, but mindful that if I dozed off, I might miss her and then not be able to talk about the show the next morning when she and I were to have brunch, I stayed awake and watched. She was terrific and I was proud to know her.

Shoptalk always; particularly at dinner parties, and one on a Saturday evening comes to mind. The guests were two psychiatrists, one businessman, two sculptors and one teacher.

After a superb meal of stuffed veal and all that went with it, one of the guests asked me if I'd read *Portnoy's Complaint.*

"Yes," I said, "and I have felt ever since that Roth should have paid me fifty dollars per hour to listen to his complaints."

Everyone chuckled affirmatives, and we talked about Portnoy. Not one in the crowd from the book business, yet it was book talk into the wee hours of the morning.

With A Book in My Hand

There have been only three times in my life when I have hand-delivered books for customers. The first two were justifiable, the third was a trial.

In the case of Peter Glenville and James Jones, there was a time problem—they were leaving the country the same night. They were staying within ten blocks of Scribner's, and somehow it was very easy to hail a cab and do a couple of nice men a favor. As a matter of fact, Mr. Jones was thoughtful enough to leave a package for me at the desk of his hotel. When I opened it, I found one of his books I had not read, and in it was inscribed: "For Celia Summer—for service above and beyond the call of duty."

All of this is by way of preface to the third delivery which put the final touch to my resolution to cease and desist.

I vividly remember the impact of Eugene O'Neill's play, *Strange Interlude*. As I read it (I was very young then), the concept of the characters speaking their lines and then revealing their true thoughts was a new experience, particularly since their innermost feelings were so remote from the words they spoke. I hadn't thought much about this quality in people until I recognized it full-blown in myself on this third occasion.

A customer I had known for some time approached me, and as she did, I suddenly wished I were out to lunch.

Celia Summer

From previous experiences with her, I had a foreboding that if I could avoid her, it would be best for us both. However, this time I was cornered. She is young and attractive, but willful and demanding—in short—a bitch. She asked me to send a copy of *The Joy of Sex* to a man who lives in Brooklyn, and to expedite it by using the United Parcel delivery service. The book therefore would arrive within a period of two or three days if destined to a New York address. In the book, she enclosed a letter which I fantasized gave instructions not only in the use of the book, but also indicated which sections to notice particularly.

As the days went by, I received daily calls from this gal complaining that her man had not received *The Joy of Sex*, and that she was beside herself. So was I, since she was about the last person I would have chosen to hassle with. I assumed from the urgency she conveyed that the missing book was presumably going to damage her relationship with this incumbent lover, and her last call was more than I could bear.

Stupidly and suddenly, without thinking, I said, "I will go home with another copy of the book, pick up my car, and deliver the book myself."

"Isn't that above and beyond the call of duty?" she asked.

"Yes," I said.

"Have you ever done this before?" she inquired.

"I did—about four years ago," I said with an artificial tone of calm in my voice, but I wouldn't reveal the circumstances.

With A Book in My Hand

"Well," she said, "it is wonderful of you."

"It's okay—think nothing of it," I assured her, lying through my teeth.

And as promised, I took the subway home on a ninety-degree summer day, picked up my car, and started to drive to Bay Ridge in Brooklyn. Since I didn't know exactly where I was going, I made a few wrong turns, and my car began to overheat. I became more and more furious with myself for falling into this trap.

Finally, I found the right address. When I rang the bell, a fairly attractive, but exasperated young man invited me in. He immediately offered me a cold drink, and apologized for what he thought was the lady's exploitation of me. Apparently, she had called to tell him of this personal delivery service.

He then explained to me that he had received a postcard from United Parcel, indicating they had tried to make a delivery, but had not found anyone at home. They requested that he call to make a date for the receipt of the book. I reassured him that I would take care of it and have the original book returned to Scribner's, if he would please accept the book I had in hand. I also promised that I would remove the enclosed letter, and mail it on to him . . . which I eventually did. He was not only distressed about the whole thing, but also quite embarrassed. On the following day, Miss Smith called to thank me for my kind gesture. She hoped it hadn't inconvenienced me too much and that I hadn't spent any of my own money to accomplish the delivery.

In a phony tone of benevolence, I said that the cost

Celia Summer

was negligible, and suggested we forget about the whole thing. I let out a sigh of tremendous relief as I hung up the receiver.

In fact, I had been neither kind nor benevolent. I had done it all just to get her off my back—to terminate the nagging of an aggressive and obnoxious human being. I must confess that when the original book was returned to me, the enclosed letter was unsealed. I was sufficiently curious to take a sidelong glance at it. The sentence that hit my eyes was as follows:

You do not really need this book. You do very well without it.

It is now ten months since I've seen or heard from her. I guess the whole experience was worth the loss of this one customer.

On a cloudless day in June, I bicycled down to the oceanfront home of a dear friend to recline in a summer lounge chair on her well-manicured lawn. Her lawn overlooks the beach—thus it is a choice spot at that time of year. We sipped iced coffee, listened to an assortment of bird calls, and from my horizontal position, I saw the full green trees against the blue sky. Suddenly time stood still. I had been hankering for this peaceful feeling for a long time.

Because she and I can talk freely with one another, I often spoke to her about things that happen at the store. She was particularly interested in the subject of best-sellers, but I was too lethargic or perhaps too complacent at the moment to explain. Now that winter has come, I am ready to search for an answer for her and for anyone else who might be interested.

One of the fascinating things for me about the retail book business is to watch a book become a best-seller, and to ask myself how it happened and why.

There is a variety of contributing factors, like a wheel with spokes, each spoke offers something to support and strengthen the wheel. Some of the factors are:

1. Book reviews
2. Word-of-mouth
3. Previous performance of an author
4. A look at a new or fresh experience
5. A new or novel "how-to" book
6. A 'Crook" book (Mafia-Vesco-Bernie Cornfield)

I should like to make it clear that no single person, no bookshop, no publisher can push a book into the best-seller category. It is something an author earns by his own creative effort, and for this he or she must be applauded. It must be obvious to most readers that some of the most successful books in the world never reach the so-called best-seller list, but have sold hundreds of thousands. Consider the great cookbooks (Julia Child's and James Beard's for example), the beautiful needlepoint, knitting, and crocheting books of Erica Wilson, Maggie Lane, the Fielding and Fodor travel guides, and most important, books written for children of all ages that go on and on in deserved popularity.

Not long ago, a few knowledgeable people put together a small book in the form of questions and answers—*How To Be Your Own Best Friend*. It took about a year for it to pyramid into a best-seller. The book filled a great need for people who wanted to know how to understand themselves.

Plain Speaking by Merle Miller, a collection of reminiscences of Harry S. Truman, came at the right time. In our post-Watergate period, reading about an honest, simple, forthright President of the United States was a refreshing experience—again a book that filled a need. So it was with Alistair Cook's *America*, a fresh look at our history at a time when we wanted encouragement and faith.

Naively, I did try to make a best-seller of a novel I loved—*The Manticore* by a Canadian author, Robertson Davies. Oh, how I tried! This novel was preceded by *The Fifth Business* for which I had tried just as hard, but failed. I still believe the author should have made the best-seller list. Perhaps, he was *too* good.

I have always believed that if I could influence the taste of shoppers at Scribner's, I would be changing a bit of the world. I have not been unwilling to try.

With A Book in My Hand

I received an advance copy of Thomas Tryon's *Harvest Home*. In it he inscribed:

For Ceil Summer—
        Who makes best-sellers all by herself.

                      Fondly,

Tom is a very dear fellow—multi-talented, uniquely handsome, an accomplished movie actor and, to top it all, he can spin some fascinating yarns. He did it again. I started and finished this one in a single evening. I was glued to my seat, paralyzed with fear, and could not tear myself away until it was all over. My note to him went something like this.

Dear Tom,
    You won't need me for this one. It's going to do it all by itself.

                      Fondly,

The fact is, I cannot make a best-seller, I don't know what made me think I could.

In the *New York Review of Books* (May 31, 1973), Gore Vidal discussed the fiction best-sellers list and wistfully wondered just who buys and who reads what sort of books. If I weren't so lazy, I would tell him!

Celia Summer

Part of the answer is in the breed of married male shoppers who stealthily enter Scribner's, snoop about surreptitiously (usually at lunchtime) and in spite of their obvious feelings of guilt about spending money, they eventually find some book or other to purchase. Their tastes are well-developed.

These men are impeccable dressers and give the air of being intellectuals. They seem, for the most part, to be successful businessmen who are genuinely addicted to books. If they read this, I hope they will recognize themselves. Sometimes they will buy children's books to make their own indulgences a little more acceptable at home. These are some of the dearest men I have ever met at my job.

While the book store was being renovated recently, many of these men had the time of their lives. They found additional excuses for visiting more often. The reason: to see how much progress was being made and to watch the changes taking place.

After all, there was some new lighting, new book stands, shifting of sections.... Some approved, some criticized, but each needed to be part of the action. The alterations at Scribner's became a "concern."

The truth of the matter is simply that the wives of these men can no longer find room for the books their husbands bring home, and so the poor souls have to resort to their own devices for appearing at home with books in hand. I can only feel that if this is their worst offense, they will inevitably be forgiven in this world or any other.

Just after writing the previous paragraph, I received a

note from one one these men. I am sure it was written with tongue-in-cheek, but it is worth the telling.

>Dear Miss Summer,
>   Could you please order the above book? Tell no one! If my wife comes in—you haven't seen me for weeks! Please call my office when the book arrives.
>
>   Thanks,
>   Jay Kaufman

I am happy to note that our female customers pretty much know what they want and are willing to accept suggestions. They exhibit no sense of guilt as they make their purchases.

It is amazing how many men and women load up on books for their airplane trips. For them, this is therapy, or as someone said, "Happinesss is an absorbing book to read to make you forget you are on a moving plane." This applies particularly to dear Josie Engel, a buyer at Saks Fifth Avenue. She demands and gets escape literature from me after she pretends to insult the daylights out of me. I have sold her more books to cover her journeys to Europe and Hong Kong than I can ever count. She, in turn, was kind enough to call a friend of mine in Hong Kong, just to say hello. It was a chore for her to locate my friend, but she did it. Josie is one of the people who makes my job a little more fun.

Celia Summer

I think one of the great satisfactions of being in the book business is the moment when someone you really care for makes the best-seller list. In one case, it was a special thrill, for Lynn Caine, then publicity director of Little, Brown, mother of two children, wrote a book called *Widow*, an honest and devastating report of what it felt like to be left with two youngsters when her young husband died of cancer.

Her bewilderment, her unpreparedness, her emotional confusion, the irrational things she did until she found herself again are an expression, I am sure, of all the experiences young widows go through. And so the book has meaning for thousands of women in America.

It was Lynn who supervised the cocktail party at which I met Han Suyin. Lynn and I have met from time to time at parties and luncheons, and when I learned she had completed a book, I prayed that it would be a success so that she could be compensated for her efforts.

On June 20, 1974, I added *Widow* to the Scribner list of nonfiction best-sellers. I hoped this book would help to give Lynn the financial security she lacked at the time of her loss.

In a seminar at college many years ago, I thought a great deal about the place of literature in my life. It was

With A Book in My Hand

clear to me even then that books communicate experience. A good book can enrich, deepen, and extend its reader's experience.

These high-toned comments are by way of a preface to a recent phenomenon. Within one week, in March 1973, we had incredibly enthusiastic reviews of *Gravity's Rainbow* by the esoteric, remote Thomas Pynchon.

Christopher Lehmann-Haupt of *The New York Times* called it "fantastic." He said that if he were banished to the moon, and could take only five books along, this would be one of them. As far as he is concerned, Pynchon is a literary treasury.

Richard Locke, of the Sunday *Times Book Review* section called it an event—the longest, most difficult, and most ambitious novel since Nabokov's *Ada*; he compared it to Melville's *Moby Dick* and the works of Faulkner.

In the *Saturday Review of Books*, Richard Poirier compared it to James Joyce's *Ulysses*. He said that Pynchon had the courage to admit that there are forms of inquiry into the nature of life that are beyond the reach of the novelist's imagination. I quote: "His novel is a work of paranoid genius that will take its place amidst the grand detritus of our culture."

Finally, Michael Wood, a teacher of English at Columbia University, admitted that the book is literally indescribable ... and very heavy going. Mr. Wood told his readers that things in the book are too often obscure, impossible to decipher, incomprehensible, yet that it is a product of a brilliant mind.

Each of these reviews became more and more com-

Celia Summer

plex as the reviewer tried to explain to us what *Gravity's Rainbow* was all about. I suspect we should have had a review of their reviews.

One day I asked Henry Steele Commager, the historian, during a visit to our store, if he planned to read the book.

"I think not," he answered, "it's too big to take to bed with me."

Then Paul Horgan, author and member of the faculty of Wesleyan University, showed up. I repeated my question. Mr. Horgan replied, "I suppose it's like a toothache—one has to endure it." However, he did not leave our store without a copy under his arm.

Finally, a very literate book salesman appeared on the scene. He said he could not even understand the reviews, so what would be the point of going further. I suspected it would be the most bought, and the least read book of the year.

All this brouhaha on my part was precipitated by a very simple thing, something that has never before happened to me: I had made several attempts to read the book. Frustrated by these aborted beginnings, I flung it clear across the living room, and I feel not one iota of remorse. With much satisfaction, I observed a falling off of sales... I really did not want to be the only one who refused to be taken in.

A direct antithesis to the fuss made about Pynchon is the insufficient attention paid to a brilliant piece written by Diana Trilling in her *Claremont Essays* on the death of Marilyn Monroe. I think of it now because of Norman

With A Book in My Hand

Mailer's big, bloated book about Marilyn Monroe. He conceded he wrote it for the express purpose of augmenting his income. In Mrs. Trilling's essay, however, I believe she came closer than any other contemporary writer to understanding this complicated phenomenon known as "Marilyn" when she said, "She was not primarily a victim of Hollywood commercialism, or exploitation, or of the inhumanity of the press. She was not even primarily of the narcissistic inflation that so regularly attends the grim business of being a great screen personality. Primarily, she was a victim of her gift, a biological victim, a victim of life itself. It is one of the excesses of contemporary thought that we like to blame our very faulty culture for tragedies that are inherent in human existence—at least, inherent in human existence in civilization. I think Marilyn Monroe was a tragedy of civilization. but this is something quite else again from, and even more poignant than, being a specifically American tragedy."

P.S. On April 19, 1974, *The New York Times* reported the goings-on at the National Book Awards ceremonies at Alice Tully Hall in Lincoln Center. To begin with, a streaker jogged through the hall shouting, "Read books! Read books!"

Then the fiction award was split between *Gravity's Rainbow* and *A Crown of Feathers* by Isaac Bashevis Singer. To compound the absurdity of this situation, Viking Press engaged Irwin Corey, the comedian who bills himself as "the world's greatest expert on everything," to make a nonsense speech, and to accept Mr. Pynchon's award. Anyone familiar with Mr. Corey's delivery will understand how confused the audience became. There were some who thought that Irwin Corey was really Pynchon, the eccentric.

All it did was to reveal that even Pynchon's publisher printed *Gravity's Rainbow* with tongue-in-cheek. I should like to conclude by quoting Steven R. Weisman of *The New York Times* who reported on the book awards.

"The appearance of Mr. Corey was evidently intended to make fun of the fact that the Pynchon novel, while hailed by critics as a work of genius, also left many of its readers confused and baffled by its encyclopedic references and intricate, fantastic style."

On May 8, 1974, a *New York Times* headline read "Pulitzer Jurors Dismayed on Pynchon." It seems that the Pulitzer committee—or jury, if you please—on fiction was utterly dismayed and disappointed by the fact that their unanimous choice for a prize for *Gravity's Rainbow* was not only turned down, but that there was no fiction award for the year.

The three jurors were Benjamin DeMott, Elizabeth Hardwick, and Alfred Kazin. I cannot think of any more distinguished critics than these. I have read them consistently, and I relish everything they have written. This is particularly ironic in that they chose a book which was simply beyond my ken. In addition, these three eminent critics received no explanation from the top echelon to make clear the reasons for the rejection.

I found it particularly interesting that the other members of the fourteen-member board, which makes recommendations on the eighteen Pulitzer Prize catego-

With A Book in My Hand

ries, had described the Pynchon novel during their private debate as "unreadable," "overwritten" and, in parts, "obscene." I never got that far.

According to the editors of *The New York Times Book Review* who chose it as one of the three outstanding books published in 1973, it was "one of the longest, darkest, most difficult and ambitious novels in years—bone-crushingly dense, compulsively elaborate, silly, obscene, funny, tragic, poetic, dull, inspired, horrific, cold, and blasted."

Mr. Pynchon could not be reached for comment.

The Scribner Building at 597 Fifth Avenue was completed in 1916, and has been designated a New York City historical site. This building houses the book store. The interior of the shop, as I saw it in 1965 with its highly polished parquet floors, the curved staircases in the rear of the shop, leading to a balcony with wrought-iron railings, and the twelve simple but elegant chandeliers hanging from the ceiling all implied dignity and superiority.

Scribner's is unique, and though I have not visited book stores throughout America, I would venture to say there is none quite like it. For, in addition to the church-like feeling created by its three-stories height, and the

Celia Summer

arched glass facade designed and created by Ernest Flagg, there *was* a certain hush difficult to describe. The atmosphere was really more like that of a library than a busy book store on New York's main thoroughfare.

Shoppers, regulars and others, spoke in whispers. Browsing was (and still is) encouraged. The smell of highly-polished floors and leather had a quieting effect ... it was a place where business or money per se seemed a secondary concern. And consequently I had the somewhat mistaken impression, during my early days at Scribner's, that most of the sales personnel did not really need to work at all. In general, these people carried an air of means about them; in several cases, it was really so.

Eight years have gone by, and I now know that most of our current employees do have to work for a living. The personnel has changed, and the store is a much busier place than it was then. For the most part, the recent renovation of the store has improved the lighting and display facilities, but the modernizing does not seem to have altered the overall impression I felt in the beginning.

In a strange and rather disturbing way, when I first came to work at Scribner's, I felt as if I had come home; this was where I belonged, in an atmosphere of books, which I loved and remembered from the days at the Abraham & Straus book department. Such an environment gave me a sense of peace, which I could never feel in my family business.

If books were my hobby, then to work with them once more seemed a delightful idea. I had never stopped

With A Book in My Hand

reading, and I could now walk into a job, still as knowledgeable as before, and make the job a creative one.

After years of being with tough men who wore dungarees and work shirts, who had one language for themselves, and another when a woman was around, I found the employees at Scribner's a well-bred lot. Here were well-dressed, meticulous men and women who seemed to know what they were doing. By contrast, the boys working as shipping clerks in the basement were far more loose-tongued. How often I would smile and remember the uninhibited swearing I was accustomed to hearing from the warehousemen. Almost immediately after settling into my new job, I knew I was going to stay.

But more than the civilized air, there was Igor Kropotkin, a man not to be duplicated. He gave me the impression that if he felt I knew what I was doing, he would give me the freedom to exercise my own judgment and I suppose I had been yearning for this kind of freedom for a long time. My instinct was right on the mark. He has been a marvelous boss all these years—equitable, cool, not reluctant at all to give praise when he feels it is due. Because of this attitude toward his employees, he rightfully receives a respect from us that is almost indescribable—no male chauvinist is he!

I suspect the family feeling among us at Scribner's is something rare. When, for example, one of our crowd suffers an unexpected catastrophe—say a theft or some financial mishap, we will make a collection to replace the loss; for the slightest occasion, someone will bake a cake ample for all.

Celia Summer

We are in the midst of everything that is new, original, and timely, and we are arrogant enough to believe our taste in many areas is pretty good. I cannot imagine any other working environment which provides as much information and mutual entertainment as our book store. I hope it goes on forever.

Our banding-together manifests itself outside the store as well. When members of the staff are invited to an author's cocktail party, we tend to group into our own Scribner circle. We should circulate, we should socialize, but in the strangest way we gravitate toward each other.

Early in 1972, a group of us was invited to a publishing party to celebrate the restaurant guide entitled *Word of Mouth*. The feast was in a ballroom at the Commodore Hotel. Ten or more food tables were prepared, each representing a foreign restaurant in New York City: Indian, Japanese, Greek, Chinese, and South American.

Suspecting we were in for some delectable treats, we of Scribner's arranged that whoever among us arrived first would reserve a table for us all. I was the first—ultimately the only woman in the group. We were eight in all, and for two hours, I was spoiled rotten by seven handsome men. As they served me food and drinks most elegantly, I kept intruders from sitting at our table—so determined were we to remain a family to the last.

On another occasion, Mr. Scribner invited some of us to a splendid party for Sir Rudolph Bing on the publication of his book, *5000 Nights at the Opera*. The party was held at our book store after closing hours.

With A Book in My Hand

Naturally, it was imperative that we circulate among the guests at this party, each of us a host or hostess of sorts, and I worried about what I might say to Sir Rudolph if I were to meet him.

Then I remembered that he had accepted a position in the music department of Brooklyn College. Sure enough, as I was introduced, I popped up with, "You do honor to my borough."

"I am honored to be there," he quickly replied, and during the evening I met Lady Bing who was eager to sit, explaining that she did not care for stand-up cocktail parties. Since I had worked that day, I shared her feeling. So in the midst of all the splendor, we were practical, realistic, and entirely pleased with ourselves when we found two unoccupied chairs. I might add we do not have more than a few chairs on our balcony.

Since then, I've made a beeline for any available chair no matter what the occasion. Furthermore, let me recommend that sitting areas be provided at cocktail parties for the book people—if we are not permitted to rest our minds, please let us rest our weary feet.

Our Michael Stevens died last year. As an ardent fan of the theatre, he would certainly have agreed that the timing of his death was abominable. He would not have

Celia Summer

chosen Christmas to remind us of the fragility of life. He would have preferred not to spoil the holiday season for us.

Michael was in charge of the biography section, and his system of maintaining it is to this day in effect. His books were not arranged by title nor by author. They were placed alphabetically by subject matter; for example, if you were searching for the book, *The Great Duke*, you would have to know it was about Wellington.

When I was still a novice at Scribner's, a gray-haired dignified lady asked me for a new biography of Robert Frost. I was having trouble locating it, and I turned to Michael and asked for help.

As if from nowhere, he took on a godlike look and arrogantly proclaimed, "You have been here long enough to know how I arrange my section!"

With a toss of his head, he walked away in disgust. The dignified lady still remembers Michael's haughtiness and his sudden act of superiority. She is Mrs. E. B. White. She thought he was awful.

I realized later on, it was just an act on his part which really didn't mean very much, but to the outsider it did not make a good impression.

Also, when I first came to Scribner's there was a clique consisting of Michael Stevens, Wendell Palmer, and Bill Troute—all attractive, and meticulous dressers. Above all, they were gentlemen.

Palmer and Troute had a special talent. They could turn on a British accent with complete aplomb. Troute would tell a customer to see the "clark" on the balcony.

With A Book in My Hand

Palmer would (after a bit of stuttering which seems part of the British manner) refer his customers to the "belle lettres" section, and I would hope the people understood French. When Troute went to lunch wearing a pair of sunglasses, a raccoon-collared coat, and dangling a cigarette from a long holder, he had the look of high society. No one would ever suspect he was a book-seller like the rest of us.

Palmer acted as if he were the host of the book store, and his specialty was turning on the charm. Sometimes he sounded like Lord Peter Wimsey, and oddly enough he resembled the actor, Ian Carmichael, in the Dorothy Sayers series on television.

When any of these three fellows vanished for a short period, it was most likely they were around the corner having a quick one. We said to anyone who asked, "Oh, they've gone to church."

Wendell Palmer is now retired, but he has taken with him many key Jewish words and phrases that I taught him and which he can use appropriately. For example, if he found me dusting books vigorously, he would say, "the *balebostah* is at work again," (the word means a capable housekeeper.) Since he was a connoisseur of foods, I taught him to use the word *"mavin"* correctly.

It was great fun to stand by and watch this "elite" group in action, and now they are all gone from Scribner's.

Michael had been with Scribner's for more than twenty years, and over the years had acquired certain fixed patterns of behavior. I knew he lived alone with his

Celia Summer

Siamese cat, Suki, whom he adored. I visited his apartment only once. It was a sort of forced visit since our group had been to a cocktail party, and Michael—who could never hold his liquor—was so drunk that we felt it was risky to leave him alone. Two of us delivered him home and we met Suki.

When sober, he was very bright. He made elaborate plans for retirement, and what with some stocks and bonds and his pension, he felt he would make it. He did not live to retire.

One of his greatest pleasures in Scribner's was to spot a lady wearing a grotesque hat. By certain signs and symbols, he would communicate the lady's presence throughout the store so that we could all share in the delectable sight.

Although he bragged about the amount of spaghetti he consumed, he always looked like a skeleton covered by clothes. Like the actor, Ray Walston (whom he resembled), he had an impish look with a wit to match. When you've watched a man with predictable patterns day after day—the coffee breaks, lunch, wisecracks, and daily periods of bickering and teasing—his absence is profoundly felt. Who will ever again call me his plum pudding pie or his deep-dish apple or sweet bird of middle age? Who will say pontifically when I am going to lunch, "Go with God, my child!"

Michael Stevens was a man who could finish your unfinished crossword puzzles with an adeptness that was incomparable, a man who could spell practically any word in the dictionary, a man who knew the entire history of

With A Book in My Hand

the motion picture industry, who played any role without a moment of hesitation. He could also remember the words to most Cole Porter tunes. He was a veritable reference book without benefit of a formal education. And most of all, Michael never let an unkind word about his fellow workers pass through his lips.

On March 14, 1973, a new book by Cecil Beaton appeared—his memoirs of the 1940s. Without blinking an eye, I said to Fran Hayden (with whom Michael and I had worked all along), "You'd better send a copy to Michael wherever he is; you know it's just his cup of tea!"

She smiled, nodded. She understood.

Wherever you are, Michael, we want you to know we won't see the likes of you again nor hear you challenge us to use the word horticulture in a sentence, and without waiting for an answer add blithely, "You can lead a horticulture, but you can't make her think."

Recently, Mrs. Paul Mellon asked me if I had known Mr. Wilcox. He worked in Scribner's children's section in the days when Mrs. Mellon left her little boy there while she browsed through adult books. She knew her son would be safe with Charlie Wilcox overseeing things.

Charlie Wilcox's name is like a thread woven through the fabric of my days at Scribner's. Legend has it that he

Celia Summer

was one of the most outrageous and pompous, but also one of the most professional, book-sellers in New York.

Many Scribner people had referred to Mr. Wilcox so often that I developed an unusually strong curiosity about this colorful fellow. I wanted to know what he looked like, how he behaved at the job—in short, what was so special about him.

Almost unconsciously, I began to question the old-timers of Charles Scribner's Sons. Luckily enough, John Hall Wheelock, my favorite Scribner poet, ambled into the book store while I was in the throes of my quest, and all I had to do was to raise the question, "Mr. Wheelock, did you know Charlie Wilcox?"

"Did I know him?" he shouted. "How could I not have known that arrogant one?" He took a deep breath and then added, "Charlie Wilcox suffered from a superiority complex and furthermore his relationship with his customers was incredible. I remember a woman who was about to choose a novel when Mr. Wilcox stopped her and said, 'You don't want that one. I'll give you the best goddamned book you ever read.' With that, Mr. Wilcox reached for the shocker of the season."

I've been told Ethel Barrymore would pull up in front of the store in a limousine, have her driver honk the horn, and out would come Mr. Wilcox with the book he thought she should read. Women believed in his literary judgment—the women of the carriage trade, that is—Mrs. Cole Porter, Marlene Dietrich, Mrs. Harrison Williams, Marcia Davenport, Edna St. Vincent Millay. Actually, he adored all avid readers. As a matter of fact, it was Wilcox

With A Book in My Hand

who chose Ernest Hemingway's reading material; and if Hemingway did not follow his advice, Wilcox fussed and fumed.

Charles Wilcox and Ernest Hemingway shared a strong interest in prizefighting, and they were good friends. One day, Faith Cross, who managed the telephone desk, received a call from Mr. Hemingway. She took it for granted that Hemingway wished to speak with Wilcox who was in another part of the building. She dialed Mr. Wilcox and said to him, "Mr. Hemingway is on the phone here. Would you care to speak to him?"

"Not especially," replied Mr. Wilcox.

Miss Cross then told Mr. Hemingway that Mr. Wilcox could not be reached and she asked, "Mr. Hemingway—do you want very much to reach Mr. Wilcox?"

"Not especially," replied Mr. Hemingway.

Mr. Wilcox worked at Scribner's from 1919 until retirement thirty-seven years later. He *was* arrogant, and it is said that he would not even have a drink with F. Scott Fitzgerald.

Charlie Wilcox was a short, stocky man with bushy eyebrows. He addressed his closest friends not by their first names, but always as Mr. or Mrs. or Miss. An unusually literate man, he was familiar with most of the authors of his time.

I've been told that Mr. Wilcox could sell any book to anyone. His word was gospel, and his enthusiasm was highly contagious.

After Burroughs Mitchell, a dear Scribner editor, read

Celia Summer

a short speech I had written, he turned to me and said, "The highest praise I can give you, Celia, is to say that Charlie Wilcox would have approved."

It is interesting that in response to my queries about Charlie Wilcox, I received a strange assortment of characterizations. One person said he was a pouting pigeon, another said he was a peacock, and still another called him a bantam rooster who could crow. In spite of these appellations, they all loved the old bird.

Incidentally, with all his formality, I am told he was not above pinching the female derrière on occasion.

The fact is, he loved Scribner's, and I've been told by Igor Kropotkin that Wilcox sold more books than anyone in the history of the book store. In truth, he managed to match the right book with the right customer.

One day, a lady walked into the shop, stared at Charlie Wilcox, then walked over to him and said, "It's a great privilege to meet you, Governor Lehman."

"Senator, madam, not Governor," replied Mr. Wilcox who in fact did resemble Herbert Lehman.

When, in the fifties, he retired, he simply went on vacation, and at the end of it, he wrote a letter announcing his retirement. It was not in his character to want a farewell party.

I am so sorry I never knew him. I was told that he concealed the fact that he had one glass eye. He was such a dapper dresser and moved with such confidence, no one could have ever suspected.

His humor was loved and remembered.

Although born in Rhode Island, he lived most of his

With A Book in My Hand

adult life in an East Side apartment with a ferocious Airedale. It is also said that he had a great appreciation for tomcats. When he saw one on the street, he would say to it, "Good hunting to you, sir."

I understand that if he liked a book, a sale of one hundred copies was assured for he merely mailed them to his customers, and there were no returns.

Charles Wilcox died several years ago at the age of eighty-seven in Vermont.

Several of us from Scribner's entered a handsome room at the Plaza Hotel to celebrate yet another novel by a liberated young woman. As was our routine, a member of the group claimed a table strategically situated to give us a prominent view of the comings and goings. As always, the Scribner people were greeted most cordially, it being somehow thought that we could do a good sales job with a book if we were so inclined. The food was superb, the drinks were more than adequate, but as I looked around I became unhappily aware of subtle changes in the book world.

Our group consisted of the younger set at Scribner's. No more the sophisticated Michael Stevens, the smooth and charming Wendell Palmer. Now, I was the senior member, and it was up to me to say who was who at the

Celia Summer

party. The author's husband, a doctor, was dressed in a turtleneck sweater and elevated shoes—certainly not the conservative apparel of doctors in my day.

The guests drifting in stretched their necks to see who was there. I did not recognize a young woman wearing a long black silk skirt, silver shoes and silver bag to match—and a patched blue denim jacket! Later, I discovered she was a poet of some distinction. They seemed to dress in costume, these young successfuls.

I suppose only in this era would we see a well-known women's lib leader amble in wearing leather gaucho pants and cowboy hat to match, or young men in velvet suits and Indian bands around their heads.

A young novelist breezed in, and we greeted each other. She sat down for a moment and asked if the mother of a certain young writer I knew was as much of a bitch as her daughter claimed. I heard myself answering, "Of course."

As I watched this charade, my mind jumped back to my early days in the book business when Mr. Scribner invited several of us to a cocktail party held at Scribner's for Marcia Davenport to celebrate the publication of her book *Too Strong for Fantasy* (a personal account of music, literature, and politics in America and Europe over half a century). It was my first, and it remains the finest party I participated in at the Scribner Book Store.

We had closed the store at 5 P.M. The porters came in to clean up and to vacuum the rugs. Every book was in its proper place. Then the French caterers took over. With efficiency and speed, they set tables with elegant white tablecloths and candelabra. Bars appeared from nowhere before you knew it, waiters in handsome red jackets moved in with hot and cold hors d'oeuvres. Elegantly dressed guests arrived. They were primarily people connected with the Metropolitan Opera House, and good friends of Mrs. Davenport. Some of us worried about the possibility of drinks spilled over the books, but that never happened. Every guest behaved with the utmost decorum. They were the kind of people who would not drink more than they could hold. In short, a totally adult group. It was undoubtedly the most elegant cocktail party I had ever been to.

At the time, I had as a customer a little lady who adored Marcia Davenport. One day, she had come into the store with several original Victor recordings of Mrs. Davenport's mother, Alma Gluck, the famous operatic singer. The records, arias from operas, were of Caruso vintage and had sold well in their time. The lady begged me to deliver them to Mrs. Davenport, and I did so at the party. Mrs. Davenport was deeply touched by the thoughtfulness of my customer and sent her a thank-you letter. The lady was overjoyed at the receipt of the letter, and paid me a visit later to tell me so. I have not seen her since.

Shortly after the Scribner party, Mrs. Davenport kindly gave me a pair of tickets to a performance of *Die Meistersinger* at the Lincoln Center Opera House.

The seats were splendid. We enjoyed every moment. I will never forget that cold winter evening with new fallen snow turning Lincoln Center into a fairyland, and

Celia Summer

the Spanish diplomat, who frequently bought books from me, offering us a lift home in his limousine cast a spell on the whole evening. The book world—there is nothing quite like it.

About five summers ago, F. Scott Fitzgerald's granddaughter, Eleanor Lanahan, came to work with us during her summer vacation. It is not necessary to say that she had inherited the fine features of her grandparents, all I need say is that an unusual number of young men suddenly came into Scribner's to browse, and to try to win a date with Bobbie (her nickname). She was an excellent worker, and as we got to know each other, the age difference seemed to dissolve.

One day Bobbie came to work with a portfolio of paintings and drawings that she wanted me to see. Her work was whimsical, ingenious, and comic. I took the liberty of showing her portfolio to Scribner's juvenile book editor, Elizabeth Shub, and in no time Bobbie contracted to do her first illustrations for a new children's book.

Bobbie was thrilled by the idea of doing a book. To thank me for my efforts, she presented me with a drawing she had done on a sunny afternoon in Central Park—a group of children picnicking while birds swooped down to peck at their balloons and a turtle happily nibbled at a sandwich. In the background were skyscrapers and penthouses all in proper proportion, and all this was done in fine lines and pastels. I was so delighted, I in turn gave Bobbie a reclining nude I had done in Venetian glass tile and to which she had taken a fancy when she came to visit my apartment.

She worked hard that summer and was excited at the prospect of the book Scribner's was going to publish. She had the kind of sweet shyness that made her try to conceal from the rest of the employees the fact that her mother dispatched a limousine to pick her up at the store in order to expedite her journey to the airport for a weekend visit home.

When she went back to Sarah Lawrence for the fall term, she asked me to visit with her, and it was a pleasantly nostalgic feeling for me to spend a day at college again.

I would add that there was only one time in our summer days together that Bobbie would have gladly bopped me over the head. A woman began an argument with me about a book she imagined was written by F. Scott Fitzgerald. I kept insisting there was no such book, but she became more and more belligerent. In desperation, I said, "If you don't believe me, ask this young lady. She's the granddaughter of F. Scott Fitzgerald."

Bobbie turned all colors, but managed to confirm my statement.

In May 1972, I received an announcement—beautifully designed by Bobbie herself—of her marriage.

The wedding took place at her mother's Georgetown

Celia Summer

house. Her father, Samuel J. Lanahan, gave his daughter in marriage, and *The New York Times* mentioned Bobbie as an illustrator of children's books. Was I ever proud!

I drove leisurely up the Palisades Parkway one morning, diverted so completely by the autumn colors (you know the big show that leaves put on at this time of the year—just like the Rockettes at the Radio City Music Hall before the curtain comes down), it was a miracle that kept me on a straight path or perhaps it was the inordinate sense of discipline I maintained knowing I had a death weapon to control.

I managed to cross the Bear Mountain bridge and wend my way to the country home of my friend Barrie Berns who will be having a book published soon—a study of widowhood in America. We'd met in the book store and, little by little, over coffee and lunches, became friends. This was my first visit, and it turned out to be a beautiful day in the country, relaxing with good, warm people. We walked through the woods. We played tennis in the afternoon and Scrabble by an indoor fire later on; and then we ate and drank, engaged in interesting conversation which inevitably led to the woes and pitfalls of writing a book and trying to get it published.

Then I began to tell my friend's family—her son and

With A Book in My Hand

her niece—about a new book I had just skimmed through—*Ego Speak*. I think it is a very bright and revealing book. The authors show us how people really don't listen to each other when they try to communicate. There is such a deep need for each one to show off or to speak that the one cannot wait for the other to stop talking so that he can get the floor.

But, how about real communication? Should we not really listen to one another without constant interruption? Shouldn't we make some effort to understand? I remember sometime back reading a wonderful book entitled *Friendship as Psychotherapy*. The thesis was that sometimes truly good friendship can help when trouble arises. At least, you might save the forty-dollar fee for the fifty-minute hour.

As I drove home in the twilight in a rather relaxed fashion, for the first time in my life I saw a deer at a "Deer Crossing." A young doe leaped across the road with the grace of a ballerina, and I thanked the Lord I was not in a hurry at that moment. As far back as I can remember, I have hoped for such an experience. I not only consider it a good omen, but a relief not to have injured such a beautiful creature.

Business at the store was to go on as usual in the spring and summer of 1973 despite the renovating. The

Celia Summer

goal was to improve store lighting, modernize the wall fixtures and the display book racks without impairing the elegant traditional look of the store and without affecting the thirty-foot-high vaulted ceiling which is one of the most beautiful interior spaces in the city of New York.

It worked! Instead of the old heavy tables, we now have modern pyramid-shaped oak fixtures that provide us with much more room to display our books face out.

The strangest part of all this was that business did go on as usual (or almost). Regular customers came in partly to buy books and partly to check on our progress. They enjoyed the changing scene just as much as sidewalk superintendents do as a new building rises. The advantage the customers had was that they could walk away from the noises, and we could not. We were stuck with the irritating sounds. I became increasingly sensitive to noise and, toward the end of the renovation period, I felt a strange internal jumpiness.

Although everything was planned and executed with considerable intelligence, we first had to endure the noise and the dust, as the wall shelves were ripped down to expose the bricks of the building. While the walls were being torn apart by one group of men, another group began to use high-velocity staple guns to alter the electric system, and the dust flew in gales.

There was always the shifting of books, and sections would disappear temporarily; sledgehammers were used to break up the old tables so that they could be carried out of the store. I was sorry to see those tables go; they had served so well for so long.

Because of the constant use of electric drills, we could

With A Book in My Hand

hardly ever hear the phones ringing, conversations were almost impossible, and in the midst of all this, customers kept drifting in and walking into areas that were roped off.

In addition to all that, new carpeting was laid in some areas and new wall racks were installed; books were carried up and down between the basement and the main floor whenever space was needed. There was much commiseration by customers wondering how we could manage to work as we did. We simply became accustomed to daily changes. But there were times when we didn't quite remember where we had placed our fiction or biography, and we had to make endless searches for requested books.

It began to be a game that consisted of coping with drastic changes plus odd and shocking noises precipitated by electric drills, staple guns, and sledgehammers. Those who were allergic to dust suffered the most.

Toward the end, when the floors had to be repolished, and everthing was moved to the side to expose the floor surface, the place took on the look of a beautiful ballroom, and all we needed was the music of Johann Strauss to envision couples waltzing freely.

My own experience was rather strange, for each night as I went home to my own peaceful apartment, I became more and more sensitive to footsteps and noises coming from the apartment above. Each day the noises grew louder. I had to request that the people above me please walk more quietly.

I am sure they thought I was absolutely mad since

Celia Summer

their footsteps had not bothered me before. It wasn't until some time after the renovation that I realized that noise pollution had temporarily done me in. Normally, the book store is almost as quiet as a library.

A year has gone by, and the nightmare is a memory. Now we are accused by Joe Dennehy, the irascible but also lovable manager of the basement, of running a country club. We are more efficient but certainly not automated. The place seems fluid, but not staid. We know where everything is, and we are still essentially the same Scribner's as before. For this, we give thanks.

As I was reading *The Life of Emily Dickinson* by Richard B. Sewall, I discovered that *Scribner's Monthly* existed as far back as 1874. It took me back countless years when I had read and devoured that dignified publication avidly at the public library each month. F. Scott Fitzgerald and Ernest Hemingway were very remote, and yet I somehow felt that *The Sun Also Rises* was one of the most perfectly integrated novels I had ever read. I had the same feeling about Edith Wharton's *Ethan Frome*.

I could never imagine that the day would come when I would be invited to Mr. Charles Scribner's apartment to help celebrate a book of photographic recollections of

With A Book in My Hand

Zelda and F. Scott Fitzgerald, by Scottie Fitzgerald Smith. By this time, I had gotten to know Scottie as Bobbie Lanahan's mother—a mother who had a very special and talented daughter. Mary Hemingway was there, too. We had met several years ago when I began to take care of her Christmas gift books list. Now, Mrs. Hemingway was working hard on her autobiography which was to center on her life with Ernest Hemingway. She was considering the proper title for her book and I was pondering one for my own. She made some suggestions for mine, but I could not respond well—I'd had two Bloody Marys. We both thought that my being published by Scribner's would be slightly incestuous. I really felt I would be lucky if anyone wanted my book.

Since Scribner's is one of the oldest and most prestigious book stores in New York, it attracts people from all over the world. Almost anyone who has written a book will stop by just for the fun of getting a glimpse at his own creation, and also to observe how well it is displayed.

This was how I met Shirley MacLaine. Her book *Don't Fall Off The Mountain*, began to do very well, ultimately reaching the bestseller list. Shirley had a certain innocence about the whole experience which was most refreshing. It is as if she couldn't believe it was happening to her, and I suppose her warmth and excitement about the writing experience was contagious. I began to enjoy her success vicariously.

The amusing part of this was that each time Shirley stopped to visit and to chat a while with me, some of my co-workers would invent sudden important reasons to address themselves to me so that they could receive an introduction to Miss MacLaine. I must say she was always considerate, polite, and totally civilized.

On one chilly morning, a large group of men and one woman entered the book store; they were cold and told us they were having a platform built outside the store for a scene of a movie. As I looked at this slim, beautiful woman in black cape, black wide-brimmed hat, with very fair skin and light blue eyes, I began to think of the Ingmar Bergman films—then it came to me. Just as she was about to ask me for *Jonathan Livingston Seagull*, I said, "You have to be Liv Ullmann." I think she liked the fact that I knew her, and we both smiled. I had seen her in several Swedish films, and was aware of her extraordinary ability to communicate sensitive, delicate experiences.

I suggested she sit on my stool and wait until she was called. She immediately became absorbed in reading the Seagull book, and forgot about her surroundings except when she was interrupted by the men in the crew who bought her a number of gift books. Their treatment of her was almost reverential, but I felt she was totally unassuming, direct, and devoid of any affectations. She really was a pleasant surprise that morning.

When Katharine Hepburn was starring in the produc-

With A Book in My Hand

tion of *Coco* in New York City, she came by one day to pick up a handful of books which, she claimed, would help her to relax between performances. She was dressed, as usual, in boots, slacks, trenchcoat, and conductor's cap. Her blue eyes shined as brightly as ever, and her face had a wind-burned look.

She asked me to choose a few books that might have a relaxing quality, and I did. Suddenly, she reached for a novel; she asked, in that wonderfully imperious manner of hers, if we should also include it. I hesitated.

"You have a blank expression on your face," she remarked.

"I will not commit myself to an opinion of a book with which I am not at all familiar," I said.

We stared at each other, and then she said, "Let's look at the art books."

As we did, she told me she was an amateur painter, but she seemed to denigrate her work. Under pressure, she said she occasionally sold a canvas for a fixed price of five dollars to Spencer Tracy. I told her that I, too, did pictures—not in paint—but in mosaics using Venetian glass tiles which I cut up into quarter-inch squares.

"How do you do it? What is your method?" she inquired.

She seemed genuinely interested, and I was only too happy to explain. I also added that I did not enjoy selling my work because when I did, I regretted it and had a real feeling of loss.

That evening, as I approached the subway, I saw Miss Hepburn's face on the cover of one of the popular

Celia Summer

women's magazines—the subtitle was: "A Portfolio of Katharine Hepburn's Paintings." I bought it immediately. I was impressed and felt that she had understated her accomplishments. I decided to send her a note of praise plus a color photo of one of my better productions in mosaic.

Soon after, I received the following note which I framed and which I love:

Dear Celia Summer,

Yours is wonderful—Oh no—never give them away—it's great just to stare at one's own genius—I'm afraid that mine look far better photographed than in reality—But I'm glad you were impressed—so was I.

Signed
K. Hep

In *The New York Times Book Review* of April 14, 1974, Rebecca West, a writer I find one of the most distinguished in the English-speaking world, wrote a stimulating review of a book entitled *Conundrum* by Jan Morris. One would have to exercise much restraint to keep from reading the book, and of course I read it the

With A Book in My Hand

very next day. It was fascinating, sensitive and truly a "conundrum."

By virtue of hormone treatment plus surgery, James Morris, journalist, travel-writer, foreign correspondent, became Miss Jan Morris at forty-six years of age. Although married and the father of four children, Mr. Morris went through his changes in total accord with his wife.

Then on June 6, 1974, Jan Morris walked into the Scribner Book Store. Since I had seen several photographs (before and after) it was not at all difficult to recognize her. Like most authors, she was interested in knowing how well her last book was doing—the one she wrote as James Morris. She was wearing white slacks, a red blouse (her small breasts were noticeable), and outside of a shadowy look around her chin (I suppose the result of a lifetime of shaving) one would not know she had been a man.

I gave the appropriate answers, but I realized after she had left how acutely uncomfortable I had felt in her presence. This was my first experience with a person who had changed sexual identity, and it was then that I realized I behave one way with women and another with men. This little encounter was fortunately brief. It was far more than I could handle. Indeed, it was a conundrum.

And yet, when Jan Morris stopped in to visit again, a week later, I was no longer uncomfortable. I found her to be warm, sensitive, gracious, and very friendly. I was now dealing with another woman, and laughter and talk came easily.

Celia Summer

Since our original meeting, Jan Morris has visited twice—this last time to say goodbye. She was leaving for England. These last visits were comfortable, felicitous, fun, and filled with pleasant conversation.

Amost everyone who works with me wanted to know what we talked about. My answer to them was that our chat consisted of impersonal observations about books, publishers, the overwhelming flies in Canada, the dullness of Toronto, sleeping or not being able to sleep on an overnight flight, and the people we knew in common. I asked that Ms. Morris send my love to Professor Rowse and Sir John Wheeler-Bennett when she arrived home. She feels about them the way I do.

My young co-workers made a collective decision that my talents lie in the public relations field. In that case, I am where I belong.

I met Jacqueline Susann and her husband Irving Mansfield in 1969 when she wrote *The Love Machine*. She was one of the first authors to say to me, "I want you to read my book," and she proceeded to pay for a copy of it, inscribe it, and present it to me.

From then on, the Mansfields would stop in to visit and chat. Once Jackie and I even planned a bike ride together. Another afternoon, they told me about an evening when Marilyn Monroe kept them waiting for

With A Book in My Hand

hours for a dinner date. I, in turn, mentioned the marvelous essay on Marilyn Monroe by Diana Trilling in her book, *The Claremont Essays*. Immediately, Jackie asked me to order a copy of the book for her. She was so eager to know and learn about everying. That afternoon I learned of her love and compassion for animals—something she shared with Doris Day—her good friend. Both women had taped a show with Merv Griffin which was solely dedicated to animal adoption—saving the lives of stray dogs. There were several dogs on the show, too. The program turned out to be one of the funniest television shows I had ever seen. Since animals know no other way of behaving but natually, the show turned out to be an absolute delight, and Jackie and Doris Day probably succeeded in saving more dog's lives that evening than is accomplished by the more serious attempts such as fundraising campaigns.

Occasionally, I would meet Jackie on Fifth Avenue with her new poodle, and tease her about the dog's ribbons and its painted toenails. She always replied that she had just come from the dog beauty parlor.

When my friends at Scribner's minimized Jacqueline Susann for being an inadequate writer, I became almost childishly defensive. I argued that she was an honest writer, wrote what she knew, stole from no one, and that she was smart enough to sell her book to the movie moguls for a million dollars.

In 1973, I gave Jackie a book which I thought she would like since it was similar to her own books. This is the note she sent to me:

Celia Summer

Dear Celia,
   Thank you so much for the book. It's thoughtful friends like you who make being an author fun. Because if I hadn't written a few books—we never would have met. Happy bike riding—Irving joins me in sending love.
                              Jackie

I am sorry that she and I never got together for that bike ride we vaguely planned together.

In 1967, my second year at Scribner's, I spotted a new novel, *Hedgerow,* by Florence Engel Randall. I couldn't believe it. My co-worker at Abraham & Straus—the dignified Florence Engel whom I called Engie (pronounced Aingy)—the gal I hadn't seen for twenty-seven years had written a book. I turned to the back jacket and happily discovered she lived in Great Neck, Long Island.
   That night I called her. "Engie," I inquired as I heard the familiar voice.
   "What did you say?" she asked incredulously. She must have remembered that I was the only person who called her "Eng."
   "Mike, is that you? I can't believe it!"

"It sure is," I gurgled.

"Where are you, Mike?"

"I'm here in Brooklyn, but I work at the Scribner Book Store now, and I found you again."

We giggled like silly young girls again; we were happy and alive.

"When can I see you? Can you come for dinner this Sunday?" she asked.

"I'd be delighted."

"Fine," she said, "I will look forward to it."

I learned later that Florence was too excited to cook. Good cook though she is, we ate Colonel Sanders' Kentucky Fried Chicken. I was nervous, too. Could we still be good friends, or had we changed after all those years?

Well, it was a happy occasion—especially after a couple of scotches and soda. I knew her husband, Murray, when he was courting Eng. Now, I met her three children, her first grandchild, and her special pet, Seymour, the cat. We never seemed to stop talking.

I was in the retail end of the book business and my friend had learned her craft well. *Hedgerow* was her first novel. As a matter of fact, it was because of our reunion and my eventual meeting with her dear literary agents, Joan and Theron Raines, that I was persuaded and encouraged to write about life at Scribner's.

In the years that have followed, her family was discreet enough to always give us a little time alone together so that we could have "book talk." Even when we went cruising in her motor boat along the North Shore of Long Island, we talked books.

Celia Summer

I was amazed that Eng could raise a family, be a loving mother and wife, and still retreat daily to her lovely "writing" room that looked out on hundreds of trees. Her only companion in the writing room was Seymour the cat, a big, handsome gray-and-white genius who sat on a stack of manuscripts to supervise his mistress's labors.

I must also add that never in my life have I ever met a more spoiled and indulged animal. To this day, I cannot get over the fact that Seymour would not eat unless someone began by hand-feeding him, then he would continue on his own.

To fill myself in on the years when we hadn't seen each other, I started to read Eng's short stories. The story which still has the greatest impact on me is called *The Watchers*. It was first printed in *Harper's* magazine, but has since been included in six short-story anthologies. Eng, *my* friend, is included in collections with Joseph Conrad, Saul Bellow, William Faulkner, Bernard Malamud, and Eudora Welty.

The murder of Kitty Genovese in Forest Hills a number of years ago left Engie with a sense of horror. According to the newspapers, Kitty Genovese was stabbed to death near her home late one night. Her neighbors heard her screams, but for some inexplicable reason, no one came to her aid. Eng was so profoundly affected by the indifference of society that she wrote a short story on the subject. It is an extremely powerful story; I can only compare *The Watchers* with Shirley Jackson's *The Lottery*.

This mature, knowledgeable and accomplished woman—a good mother, grandmother and excellent wife—seems to possess limitless love for every living thing. I remember a telephone call when her voice was cracking and sobbing because Seymour was sick, at the veterinarian's, and "if anything happened to Seymour, she would not know what to do."

Fortunately, Jeffrey showed up—another gray-and-white cat. He became number two. However, Seymour, when he had recovered, decided he didn't like this at all. He was so furious and so jealous that he refused to eat for four days until Eng picked him up in her arms, shed a few tears, and begged, "Seymour, you know I still love you, please eat your food?" And he did.

Jeffrey had come at the right time. Seymour, at fourteen years of age, had become spiteful and suffered poor digestion. He was not fast enough anymore, and a passing car killed him. Eng was much better about Seymour's demise than I thought she would be. But we all missed him.

Since *Hedgerow*, Florence has written several more novels—two books for young adults, and many short stories. I must add that when she presented me with her British edition of *Hedgerow*, she wrote:

> For Mike—who is one of the unexpected and delightful bonuses of *Hedgerow*
>
> > With love,
> > Florence

In her novel, *Haldane Station*, Eng needed five female names, so she used my proper name and those of

Celia Summer

my four sisters. In September 1973, she presented me with the new book and wrote:

For Celia—
    Who is one of my favorite characters—
        With all my love,
        Florence

Florence Engel Randall is still as disciplined as ever in her writing. Her attitudes are wholesome, and her compassion is extensive. I hope we can go on for a long time with our "book talks." If it weren't for Scribner's, I might not have rediscovered my old friend. For this, I am most grateful.

On Wednesday, July 3, 1974, I gratefully entered the air-conditioned bus that takes me home. I sat down and looked at the headlines of the *New York Post* ... "Rockefeller Aide Dies in Plunge on East Side." I read further, "Former Governor Rockefeller's executive assistant plunged to her death today from the 10th floor bedroom of her East Side apartment." Then the name came—Louise Auchincloss Boyer.

Tears started to roll down my cheeks, and I had difficulty concealing this from the other bus riders. She

With A Book in My Hand

had just visited me the day before at the book store to pick up some copies of a book on the landmarks of New York by her friends, Martha Dalrymple and Harmon Goldstone, and was on her way to Martha's place for lunch. They were preparing a vacation trip to Africa.

As I kept wiping the streaming tears, I was struck by the notion that ours was a very special relationship that could only have developed between a book-seller and a lady of charm, wit, and character. It had been at least five years that we had been gently and lovingly insulting each other. Mrs. Boyer started it.

At Christmastime, she and the other ladies of the Governor's office at 30 Rockefeller Plaza did much shopping for themselves and the Governor. Perhaps they had missed me once or twice and so after that they would phone and ask, "Will you be there or will you be out lunching—it seems to us that you are forever eating."

Patiently, at first, I reminded them I was entitled to lunch. Then I indicated the time I would definitely be available. God only knows the qualities with which they endowed me, but I fell into their pattern very easily. After Louise Boyer had kept these inferences going for a while, I decided to get even. Her nephew, Philip Boyer, had written a novel called *Sidelong Glances of a Pigeon-Kicker*. From then on whenever I received a message that Mrs. Boyer had called, I would return the call with "Is this the aunt of the pigeon-kicker?" And she would reply, "Of course, and by the way, have you been out stuffing yourself with goodies?"

When she walked into Scribner's, I would put on a

Celia Summer

look of bewilderment, and say (only for her ears), "Oh my God—the enemy is approaching."

I must say, at this point, that Governor Rockefeller's office had a collection of some of the most sophisticated, charming, and intelligent women I have met. What is more, they exuded a collective kind of humor which the world could use more of.

I don't think I will ever forget the innumerable verbal attacks I received from them (particularly Louise) about my eating habits. I admit they were all slim (probably lived on cottage cheese), but they had to eat sometime, or else they dieted more vigorously than I could ever do.

Since Mr. Boyer died about two years ago, Louise suffered more than one heart attack, but made light of each. She implied laughingly, that her home away from home was the Columbia-Presbyterian Hospital and even showed me her hospital credit card. When I sent her a novel to read while she was recuperating, her thank-you letter was signed: "Louise (Pigeon-kicker's aunt.)"

Not so long ago, I had read and enjoyed Fawn Brodie's biography of Thomas Jefferson. I thought Louise would like it, and (I don't do this often) I met one of her friends and begged her to drop it off at 30 Rockefeller Plaza for Louise. Her thank-you to me went something like this, "How could you think of weighing my friend down with a book that weighs a ton?" Later on, she admitted she loved reading it and was completely absorbed at the time.

The odd thing about all this banter was that we always kissed each other on the cheek with every visit no matter how much we kidded around. I didn't know that when I kissed her soft, slim face this past Tuesday as we said goodbye, it would be for the last time.

Oddly enough, Josie Engel, buyer at Saks Fifth Avenue, has taken up where Louise left off, but she doesn't realize it. We have the same relationship that existed between me and dear, unforgettable Louise Boyer.

I cannot quite remember how many years ago it was when Sibylle first came to browse in Scribner's. What impressed me so much was the fact that she looked like she had stepped out of the pages of *Vogue* and that she had such unusually good taste in her choice of books. I soon learned that she worked for Lufthansa airline, but I never did see her in uniform.

She began to appear at regular intervals so that I could almost sense when to expect her. One day, she breezed in and suggested we lunch together.

Sibylle was born and grew up in West Germany. When she was a baby, her father was killed in battle by the Americans. Her mother remarried, and there was a brother and sister whom Sibylle adored. It was refreshing to meet a young woman who not only respected her mother, but also considered her a dear friend. When

Celia Summer

Sibylle was old enough, she studied languages at Heidelberg. Eventually she became an airline hostess.

After our first lunch date, we began a ritual of lunching together. We ate in a Swiss restaurant. Sibylle ordered for me, and she had very good taste in wines.

Our friendship developed, but I always felt self-conscious with her about being Jewish. Finally, I told her. She said simply, "I feel no guilt." I sighed and felt better. Our friendship continued. We discussed writers from all parts of the world. She had been everywhere. She knew how to shop well in any city. She could switch from one language to another with ease, and she knew where to get the best buys for her money. With each visit to New York, she would bring me gifts—a hand-made belt from Africa, white fur bed-slippers from South America, scarfs from Paris and Peru, and even foreign champagne, and cookies from Nuremberg.

I in turn decided to supply her with the books I enjoyed, and there was great pleasure in the exchange of these gifts.

The trouble with having a friend who flew so much was that it brought a little anxiety. One morning, on my way to work, I opened *The New York Times* and read of a crash of a Lufthansa plane. As the day wore on, I became increasingly worried—I couldn't wait to get home because I knew I was going to call Frankfurt to be sure Sibylle was all right. I found it easier to call Germany than I thought. Once I heard Sibylle's voice, I was immediately relieved. She was not at all surprised that I called. She had received other calls for the same reason.

With A Book in My Hand

After that, I received cards and letters from all over the world—Switzerland, Spain, Africa, Thailand and India. It was her way of telling me she was safe.

Since Sibylle was single, she arranged to bring her mother to New York. Her mother was delightful. We saw each other all the time that she was in the city. It made my job a lot more fun than usual. It also made me look at our city through the eyes of a foreigner, and therefore interested me all over again.

Sibylle married, and recently came with her husband so that we could meet and spend time together. How we celebrated! I must confess that they knew more about good eating places in this city than I had ever known.

Sibylle retired from flying at thirty, and I must now plan to visit my friends in Düsseldorf. Until then, there will be letters, and books back and forth—and most of all—a joy in the anticipation of meeting again.

If I had thought of keeping a diary of the daily goings-on at the Scribner Book Store, I believe it would reveal a chart similar to one depicted by the Dow-Jones market reports in that our emotions fluctuate just as frequently and with valid reason.

I have a firm conviction that throughout history there have been people put on this planet for the sole purpose

Celia Summer

of torturing other people (if they are permitted to do so).

A lady walked in today, and pedantically informed Frances Hayden (one of the most experienced people working in the book store) that she had read just about everything, but did Fran have a good new book for her to read. Poor Fran was flabbergasted, but she did make a valiant effort to fill the bill even though her temper was rising to boiling point. When Fran reached her peak of tolerance, her eyes rolled upward, she almost threw up her hands, and by sheer luck she was saved by a telephone call.

Then, a new and less experienced young lady took over, and the customer gave Linda the same spiel about how well-read she was and how difficult it would be to satisfy her needs. Suddenly, I weakened. I felt so sorry for Linda that I barged in (probably with a very conscious desire to get this dame out of the store as rapidly as possible).

The lady gave me the same malarkey about her erudition. I made a few suggestions, and she pooh-poohed them. I even honored her enough to offer John Fowles's newest and finest book *The Ebony Tower*, and with complete disdain, she implied that he bored her.

Out of sheer perversity, I decided to recommend a book that I knew we were out of—Edna O'Brien's collection of short stories entitled *A Scandalous Woman*. When I pretended to look for it and obviously did not find it, she decided this book was her heart's desire. How soon could I get it? I couldn't make any promises—not at all. She was adamant. She wanted it as soon as possible. I

With A Book in My Hand

refused to make a commitment and began to enjoy this sadistic game. Unfortunately, one of our new young men overheard part of the dialogue, and without any knowledge of my diabolical behavior he popped up with, "Miss Summer, I know where there is a copy of *A Scandalous Woman*."

"Well," I said with resignation, "let's have it." He produced it and the "dear soul" bought it, and we all sighed with relief as she left. Oddly enough, I had read only one review of the book, and my self-preserving instincts must have been working because if I hadn't come up with something, we all might have begun to tear at our respective hairs.

The day was saved by the appearance of Edwin Newman of NBC-TV. His book, *Strictly Speaking*, had just arrived, and as he walked into our store (I must admit that most of us respect and admire him) I invited him to autograph his book. Like most authors, he was delighted to do so, and he enjoyed the experience like someone with a new-found toy. He was so thoroughly delighted at the thought that there were people buying his book, he made no bones about showing his appreciation. We invited him back. He made us all forget that harridan who "had read everything there was to read."

Shortly thereafter a man walked into Scribner's and challenged me, "Do you know books?"

"Yes," I responded with overconfidence. I felt like saying, "I'm not here to sell apples."

"Do you know all the books in this store?" he again demanded.

"Yes," I lied defiantly.

Celia Summer

"Well," he asked, "do you have *Lenny*?" (I really thought he was going to ask for something like *The Cambridge History of Outer Mongolia*). I gathered he meant the biography of Lenny Bruce. Without further conversation, I walked away, picked up the book, and presented it to him. He smiled apologetically and said he had been kidding. I hope he does his "thing" next time in Brentano's.

A little while later, I noticed Mr. Scribner and Alan Paton in the book store. Mr. Paton was examining a book on trees which we publish, and was defying Mr. Scribner to identify some odd-looking tree. I suggested that Mr. Paton was not fair since Mr. Scribner is essentially a city man, but I also surmised that these two men really knew and liked each other and that this was their way of gently teasing each other. It was good to see Mr. Paton again. For me, he has always been one of the great writers to emerge from South Africa.

On November 14, 1974, the firms of Alfred A. Knopf and Harper & Row invited me to a party for Sybille Bedford to celebrate the publication of her forthcoming biography of Aldous Huxley in the library of the St. Regis Hotel. I have gone to many cocktail parties for authors, but never did I find such a collection of brilliant, creative people in one room, and I will wager that it will not

With A Book in My Hand

happen again for a long time to come. First, I ran into Louis Auchincloss, then my dear friends Shirley Hazzard and Francis Steegmuller—and then, with my mouth hanging open, I was introduced to Janet Flanner and Hannah Arendt. I must admit, it was almost more than I could bear. I have a profound respect for these two women, and for a fleeting moment I felt like a child let loose among the most elegant and beautiful toys in the world.

Since I am known among my intimates as a late bloomer I am sometimes totally astonished and shocked at my behavior when I unconsciously set myself up as an authority at my job.

For example, a sophisticated, attractive, and highly successful businessman I know, who is also an avid reader, popped up the other day with four books in his hands which he had procured from what I call the "sex" department on our balcony. Two of the books were by Masters and Johnson on human sexual responses, and the other two were *The Joy of Sex* and *More Joy* by Dr. Alex Comfort.

"Ceil," he said, "a friend of mine is remarrying and since you never mislead me, please tell me which of these books is most appropriate."

Without a moment's hesitation, I eliminated the

Celia Summer

Masters and Johnson books. I declared they were a little too technical and statistical. I recommended the Comfort books on the grounds that their attitudes toward sex were those approaching a sport. Incidentally, in his book *Sex and Society*, Dr. Comfort said, "The fact of having made sex a problem is the major negative achievement of Christendom."

I then asked my customer friend if he wanted the books wrapped as a gift, and he said no—a plain sack would do. After he left, late bloomer that I am, I realized that his friend was nonexistent—that when people are embarrassed about requesting books, they always tend to attribute the purchase to the needs of friends or family. Of course, this is most forgivable, but it did remind me of the young man who was interested in books about incest because he knew a brother and sister involved in such a practice.

Shortly after this incident, John Chancellor of NBC news, stalked briskly into the store to buy the book *Total Fitness*, which was a new method for keeping physically fit with a minimum of exercise; it recommends walking upstairs instead of using elevators, lifting a heavy bag now and then and such.

"You look fit enough," I jokingly commented to Mr. Chancellor.

"Yes," he said, "I walk two miles each morning to work."

"Do you ride a bike?" I asked pedantically.

"Yes," he said, "on week-ends."

"In that case," I remarked, "I doubt you need the book."

With A Book in My Hand

We then got into a discussion of alcohol and its deleterious effects. He told me he has just one Martini before dinner. I countered with, "You'd better not— it's toxic," I said this with great authority, "I mean the combination of gin and vermouth is very damaging to the body." (I learned this from a very scientifically knowledgeable friend.)

"Well," he asked, "how about straight scotch?"

"Much better," I replied.

As a matter of fact, I told him I found that one or two Bloody Marys, at cocktail parties, are easiest for me, and they don't seem to be intoxicating in any way. I really believe that the large amount of tomato juice has a neutralizing effect upon the rest of the "gook" in the drinks.

"In any case," he said, "I'll buy the book, check it out to see if I am doing something wrong, and I will let you know." I hope he will let me know, because I am much too lazy to read a book about physical fitness. I'd much rather take a bike ride in the sun. I might add that I know very little about drinking so that my instructions to Mr. Chancellor now seem most amazing to me.

Once when I was called to the phone at the book store, a pleasant male voice announced, "my name is

Celia Summer

Stuart Little." I immediately envisioned E. B. White's little mouse come to life, and I began to laugh uncontrollably. When I finally stopped, I apologized to Mr. Little, and explained my spontaneous reaction. He understood since I am certain this has happened to him before.

Mr. Little said that he was the editor of *The Authors Guild Bulletin*, and would I please supply him with a photo of myself since the *Bulletin* was doing a piece about me at the suggestion of Roger Angell of *The New Yorker*. Then I burst out laughing again—this time illogically since Roger Angell's mother is Mrs. E. B. White, and E. B. White is the little mouse's creator. It all got a little silly.

I furnished the only black and white photo I had which might be suitable for reproduction. The picture ran in *The Authors Guild Bulletin*—Jan–Feb–March 1976 issue. Above the photo was the title "BOOKFRIENDS." Underneath it said:

> Celia Summer, of the Scribner Book Store, 597 Fifth Avenue, in New York, is a lifetime user and pusher of books, a swift and reliable advisor to book seekers, a housemother to authors. Sociable, partisan, critical, comical, she patrols her splendid corridors with the expression of one who at any instant expects to introduce the perfect reader to the ultimate author: "Dr. Johnson, this is my friend Mr. Trollope. Listen, has either of you read the new Updike?"

With A Book in My Hand

Perhaps Roger Angell wrote the copy. If so, I am afraid he is perceptive and knows me too well at my job. Some notes received afterward:

From Stefan Lorant—

Dear Celia Summer,

I loved your picture in *The Authors Bulletin*—But why so solemn? Next time—please smile—as usual—

With best regards

From the Paul R. Reynolds Literary Agency—

Dear Celia,

I loved your picture in the *Authors Guild Bulletin* and the quote is a honey. Ran all over the office with it and we all of us send you our love.

All the best,
Elsie Stern

From American Booksellers Association, Inc.—

Dear Ceil:

Congratulations on being picked as the Authors Guild first Bookfriend!

That's really nice. And deserved.

Cordially,
G. Royce Smith
Executive director

Celia Summer

A long time ago, my father's employees decided that I should have a boy's name if I were to ride on the trucks with them. They chose "Mike," and the name stuck. As I went from public school to high school to college, someone would always pop up and say loud and clear, "Hello, Mike." Finally, I gave up and yielded. I was to live with two names for many years.

When I came to work at Scribner's, I thought it was a beautiful opportunity to conceal the nickname, and I almost succeeded until I became friendly with satirical artist Robert Osborn of Salisbury, Connecticut. How could I know that Mr. Osborn was a neighbor of Arthur Miller's. How could I know that Mr. Osborn would proceed to tell Arthur about his book-seller friend, Celia Summer, and then (as I put it together) that Arthur would say to Mr. Osborn, "Her name is Mike."

Arthur is the older brother of one of my oldest and dearest friends, Joan Copeland. We've known each other for a long time, so for Arthur, I was still Mike.

Last Christmas, a large envelope was delivered to the Scribner mailroom which baffled the entire staff. It was addressed to "Mike S." in elegant artistic scrawl. Underneath my name was a hand-drawn Christmas tree.

Needless to say, the letter drove the mailroom staff crazy. The boys wandered through the entire Scribner Building, making inquiries. I don't know how long it took

With A Book in My Hand

before the staff of the book store was approached. Joe Mummery, of our mail-order department, came to me and asked, "Ceil—do you suppose this letter could have been meant for the deceased Michael Stevens?"

I blushed and answered "No, Joe, I suspect it's for me." (I had noticed the name Osborn in the upper left-hand corner.) Then I launched into a hasty explanation of why I knew the envelope was for me. My secret was out. When I opened the letter, there was a drawing of a ski accident. On the other side, it said:

M—happy new year!
This is a ski accident! like Nixon and U.S. morality!
      Signed—Bob Osborn

I wrote to Mr. Osborn, telling him how he had confused the mailroom, and would he please use my proper name in the future. And so he sent me four more: to "Celia Summer," to "the Celia Summer," to "Celia Fate," and to "Sea Summer."

I have received every letter, and now I want to thank the Scribner mailroom for their understanding.

Robert Osborn and his wife went off to Sicily recently, and he almost didn't return. He suffered an embolism, but luckily he has recoverd. I wrote him a note, and this was his response:

Dear Mike,
  Thanks for your note—also all of the bike advice (frankly I prefer walking here in the hills,

Celia Summer

jogging *gently*, and best, swimming in a small, round, deep pool beyond the glass-walled bedroom).

It was apparently a close call—had the full clot in the right leg let go—that would have been it—"Death in Venice"—However, I might have gotten to be buried next to Stravinsky and heard good, new music through the earth until Venice really went under—then whale clickings and dolphin talk.

Love,
Bob

P.S. Arthur called at once, offered to come over. How decent he and Inge are. They are well and full of laughs.

"You seem to know everything about this place," said a nice lady—she was repeating what had been told to her by people who met me at the store. Of course, I am pleased when book buyers appreciate the book-seller who knows what's between the covers of the book she or he sells. I expected the lady to request an esoteric book or an out-of-print title. After the compliment, I smiled and waited. I didn't want to rush her. It was a quiet moment. Finally, after a minute passed, she said, "I'm looking for a copy of *Chicken Licken*." I continued to smile.

"Well, yes, *Chicken Licken*, a child's story, I believe," and with these words I directed her to dear Marion Bell, our buyer of children's books, who whipped out *Chicken Licken*. As for me, I went about the store for the rest of the afternoon singing "Henny, Penny" as my niece had taught it to me years ago, when she was four. The staff begged me either to stop or to pack up my accouterments and to depart *tout de suite*.

Later that day, a fair-haired, wholesome-looking young man asked me to check *Books in Print* to see if the title he wanted was still available. Both of us were peering over the volume when I suddenly glanced down at the watch on his left wrist.

"Whoever heard of a watch with the words 'Scotch Whiskey' written clear across the face of it?" I blurted out.

"Do you like it?" he asked.

"Yes, it's silly enough for me to like it."

"In that case, you may have it."

I looked at him with shocked delight as he removed it and pushed it into my hands.

"Can I give you a book in return?" I asked.

"No, no—just take it and enjoy it."

Well, we became friends and I am still wearing his watch.

Celia Summer

There is a pleasant anticipation when we open the Scribner Book Store each morning at 9:30. Each day is so different. One doesn't know what might happen or what to expect. One morning, a call came at the telephone desk. The man at the other end said, "I wish to place an order."

"What is your name and address?" asked Faith Cross.

He gave that information.

"Would you like to charge it?" she asked.

"Yes," he replied.

"Very well then, what would you like?" she asked politely

"I would like a ham on rye with pickle and mustard and a coke," he stated.

"I am afraid you have the wrong number," Faith said, and then she burst out laughing and came to tell the rest of us about her very special order.

On arrival, we check stock for the books for which each of us is responsible and then secure replacements. There are approximately forty employees at the store. This includes our fellows in the basement who ship and receive books as they come in and separate them into categories. We might need to make one or two trips to fill our stock. With the stock arranged on the shelves for that day, work has begun.

I am in charge of history, current affairs, archaeology,

With A Book in My Hand

anthropology, and two handsome tall stands that you see on either side of the store as you enter. One stand features new books and the other display is for bestsellers. Both these stands require continual attention because they draw customers like magnets. There is constant replacement and straightening of this display. The books should look handsome, enticing, and neat!

As to procedure, each title has a card on file so that we can check immediately, if someone should request something with which we are not familiar. Strangely enough, many people know neither the author nor the title of the book they desire, but they tend to describe in this way,

"It takes place in the nineteenth century and it's about a large family," or,

"It's about four spies who don't know there is a fifth spy involved," or,

"It's about a fellow who has gone back to his native land to look for his roots," or,

"The book may be a novel or a biography about a man and his wife on an archaeological dig."

Thus our job is to know the books well enough to match the right title to the description given. Then we pray that we can trace the book.

If there are several copies of one title, then there is a yellow order slip in one of the books near the bottom of the stack. The slips for each title are piled up as the cashiers receive the books, and we in turn retrieve our slips to watch the speed of the sales, hence knowing when to reorder and how much.

Celia Summer

The original ordering of books is done by management. After that, it is up to each person in charge of a section to follow up on orders. In this manner, we have a good checkup system.

Fiction shelves are in the back of the store. Fiction was up front years ago, but it was decided that nonfiction, being more popular, should be closer to the entrance. The move seemed to reflect the current taste of book buyers.

In the very rear of the store is an extremely handsome art department. It consists of elegant art books, theatrical books, and books about the entertainment world.

On the handsome balcony of the Scribner Book Store, one can find books on psychology, nature, philosophy, the occult, transportation, sports, religion, standard authors, poetry, belle lettres (essays and literary criticism), reference, dictionaries, atlases, thesauri, science, medicine, and other technical books. We have a glassed-in section of leather-bound classics that contain very good-looking editions of the immortal books.

The busiest time at Scribner's is between 11:30 A.M. and 2:30 p.m. Many people in the Rockefeller Center area seem to enjoy spending part of their lunch hours browsing and buying.

When I first came to Scribner's, we had two types of purchases—cash or Scribner charges. Now, books can be bought with BankAmericard, American Express Cards, Master Charge, Citicard and Scribner charges. As a result, we have a more computerized system than before, but it works well in the long run.

With A Book in My Hand

On any given day, we can have laughter, aggravation, irritation, and yet there is a camaraderie among us that tends to lighten the minor burdens and make the day go faster for me than it would anywhere else. I think it is mostly fun.

I often play hostess to authors when they come into the store to autograph their books. So it was with Melvin Belli. He was to be in at 3:30 P.M. to sign copies of his autobiography just published by Morrow. For some strange reason, I said to my co-workers, "Marvin Belli will be in today, and we must make a nice display."

"Ceil, his name is Melvin not Marvin," stated Leslie Reif.

"OK, OK—I'll try to remember. I'll keep telling myself—Melvin not Marvin," I replied.

All day long, Marvin and Melvin drifted interchangeably in and out of my mind. What kind of a stupid confusion was this?

By the time Mr. Belli arrived, I did not dare speak his name. I slipped my arm in his, escorted him to a seat, and we made small talk.

As he left, he charmingly turned and said, "This is a beautiful book store. Whenever you are in San Francisco, I want you to come to see my offices. They are interesting, too."

Celia Summer

"I will, I will," I replied.

Mr. Belli, please forgive me if you happen to read this!

In 1975, Charles Scribner's Sons, Publishers, posted notices throughout the Scribner Building that there was to be a contest open to all employees to cut out, assemble, and color a house of four rooms from a special book designed by Evaline Ness. The book is intended for eight- or nine-year-old children. (As far as I am concerned, it is for all ages.) It is called *American Colonial Paper House*. Each page can be pulled from a spiral binding. The floors and walls are sturdy cardboard, easily removable from the book. The house has a kitchen, dining room, parlor and bedroom—no roof. Altogether, I would say the whole, when assembled, is a square—each room twelve by twelve inches. The diminutive furniture is to be cut and glued together from heavy paper. I thought it was a brilliant conception and a very tempting contest. It was my chance for creative play.

There were two contestants from the book store: Peggy Elwert, assistant to Marion Bell who is head of the juvenile department in the book store, and myself. Much later, I learned there were eight more contestants from the publishing side of Scribner's.

I rushed out to buy a set of colored pens. For three

With A Book in My Hand

weeks following—after arriving home and rushing through dinner—I worked on the cut-outs for the major part of each evening. I felt as if I had entered a special minature world, and I became so absorbed that nothing else seemed to matter. I was very careful in matching the wallpapers with the colors of the furniture. I made wall mirrors of tin foil and thought I was being terribly clever when I glued white buttons on the dining room table for serving plates. I even pasted a tiny porcelain dog on the dining room floor.

Every now and then I would try to pump Peggy for information about her progress, but I found her totally noncommital.

I had a considerable sense of pride when I found I was the first to submit my project to Lee Deadrick, chief editor of the juvenile books. She accepted it gracefully, with genuine praise for my work.

A day before the prizes were to be awarded, I rode up on the elevator to the board room on the eighth floor where ten houses were well-displayed on a long meeting table. My heart pounded with jealousy. Peggy had created a fireplace broom from a toothpick. On the paper bed, she had sewn a tiny patchwork quilt, on the floor was handmade oval rug. To top it off, she had tiny artificial flowers in a gold-plated vase on a little round table covered with a hand-sewn white linen cloth. I was certain that Peggy would win.

Marcia Latz had included diminutive knives, forks, artificial fruit in a bowl, artificial plants; everything in beautiful color combinations. All the others were so

Celia Summer

original and yet so different from each other that I felt I was doomed. Even the gracious praise I received from Mrs. Scribner and Mary Rodgers, author of children's books, did not make me feel better. It may have been that because Trevor Gaskin of the accounting department had placed a handsome miniature of himself (he really is handsome) over the fireplace that he won third place. Peggy was second, and Marcia was first. I was not a good loser. Yet, all these little houses (including mine) were displayed in store windows—Rizzoli's, Doubleday's, F.A.O. Schwarz, and numerous department stores with each of our names attached to our respective houses.

The second contest at Scribner's was called "A Paper Palace Contest" from Evaline Ness's book. The contestants had to cut out and color a four-room paper palace. This project was far more complex than Evaline's colonial house the year before.

The book, as the author points out, is for anyone who "cannot resist a palace." She suggests that a palace is not a palace unless it has tons of gold. Well, I could resist a palace, but I could not back away from the challenge of another try at winning. I discovered that the contest allowed us to invite members of our families to participate. I trapped my niece, Stephanie Prezant, into doing a little of the gold work.

After a week of applying gold wherever possible, finding small rugs for me from her daughter's doll house, prodding her husband into cutting tiny mirrors of as-

With A Book in My Hand

sorted sizes (his business is cutting glass and replacing it in damaged automobiles), she returned her part of the project knowing I was grateful for her contribution.

This time I decided to learn more about color before I proceeded. I planned to color the entire palace and all the furniture, and provide pictures for the walls. Unsure of the best available materials, I called a conference with Barbara Gutmann, a commercial artist who was my neighbor. Barbara, by the way, adored the work of Reynolds Ruffin, who did the art work for the Scribner Riddle Calendars.

I invited Barbara to my apartment, offered her the 1977 Riddle Calendar, and then asked her advice about paint materials. She examined the quality of the paper in the palace book, thought about it for a while, left the apartment and soon returned with a large box of seventy magic markers of every possible shade.

"Now," she said, "you have all the material to work with. Use these colors freely and speedily. They dry fast and will not streak."

Then she abandoned me, feeling she could trust me from that moment on. I finished coloring the library which was filled with books. I needed a picture over the fireplace. I went through all my albums and found the only one that seemed appropriate. It was a color photograph Sibylle had sent me of herself months earlier. In it, she was sitting in an elegant chair, sipping tea, and wearing a broad-brimmed hat that lent a regal touch to her appearance. She seemed to belong in the setting.

Celia Summer

I worked feverishly for eight nights to complete the job. I found a small artificial Christmas wreath at a Lamston's on Madison Avenue, and I couldn't resist a diminutive barrel of apples in Hallmark's window, thinking that these little touches might add to my chances.

While I was doing my shopping for the palace, I was unaware that Henrietta, my sister, was also scouting around for contributions to my enterprise.

Henrietta made a flower arrangement from Q-tips dipped in mercurochrome, added artificial leaves and placed all in a "vase" that was probably the cap of a perfume bottle. Then she bought a tiny model of a 1920 Ford, a toy 1900 Singer treadle sewing machine, a miniature bottle of Good Seasons salad dressing, and a wee Venetian-glass dachshund.

The employees in the Scribner Building were mum. I knew nothing about any of the other entries. Nobody could possibly have had seventy magic markers of every color imaginable cluttering his or her dining table, plus little rugs, scissors, and paint brushes scattered about. My table was no longer a place for dining, but I didn't care about that. I had a strange feeling that I knew more about what I was doing this time than I had the last, and even if I didn't win, it had been fun to do.

I forgot to mention that my old colonial house now graces Melissa's room. She is Stephanie's four-year-old child. It serves a good purpose since Melissa is completely enchanted with it. Fortunately, she is still too young to perceive the mediocrity of her great-aunt's artistry.

With A Book in My Hand

The following sign was posted:
A PAPER PALACE CONTEST
We are pleased to announce the judges for the Paper Palace Contest. They are Evaline Ness, and Nancy Jo Fox—an interior designer and instructor at the New York School of Interior Design.

Judging will be a 10 A.M. on November 29th, with prizes awarded in the conference room at 2:30 P.M. Please bring all palaces to the 7th floor.

On Monday, the day of the awards, Henrietta went up to the board room of the Scribner Building to see the paper palaces on exhibition. While she was enjoying the spectacle of the seven palaces on display, one more handsome than the other, a gray-haired man, wearing a tan wool cardigan, walked into the room. She said to him, "This display is just a magnificent work of art. It is so beautiful, the public should be able to see it. Why doesn't Scribner's get the television people in so everybody can view this gorgeous array, and, P. S., I'm not in any way connected with Scribner's." Surprised, the man stared at her and said, "I'll tell the publicity department."

A few minutes later I had to go up to the juvenile department on the seventh floor to retrieve some of my working materials. On my way back to the store, I met the man in the sweater whom my dear sister had so wisely counselled. Mr. Charles Scribner!

"I hear you ran into my sister in the board room," I remarked, recovering from my surprise. We chatted

Celia Summer

about what my sister had said. Mr. Scribner smiled and agreed that her point of view was a good one. He said that the publicity department had postponed the awards until the following day in order to arrange for photos and to give people and visitors more of a chance to see the paper palaces displayed so beautifully.

Another poster appeared:

Tuesday—November 30, 1976
To All Employees

You are cordially invited to the premiere showing of the models entered in the Paper Palace Contest. Prizes will be awarded at this time.

2:30 P.M.
Board Room—Eighth Floor

I showed up on time, and to my chagrin, I lost again, and I cannot pretend I was happy. In any case, it was lots of fun while it lasted.

Through the years, I have come to know the sales representatives from many publishing houses. Most of these men have become friends, and I always look forward to their visits to Scribner's. We all share a deep

With A Book in My Hand

interest—a love—for books. Without exception, the reps I have met know their books very well. On occasion, when one comes in, we might go off to a quiet corner of the store to talk about what's coming up and how things are going. We talk about how many copies of a book are being printed, which books are moving and which are not. Shoptalk is fun and always the meat of these get-togethers, which I have grown to love. More than that, I feel a personal concern for each one's success.

Sales reps are largely responsible for our being asked to the book-launching parties, but most cherished by us is their generosity in sending us advance copies of significant books on their lists. This serves a double purpose. We enjoy reading them and then can offer them in a knowledgeable way to our customers.

Louis Auerbach, who is a free-lance rep, is a delightful man—"the Jewish leprechaun" as he is known in the trade. He was formerly sales manager and vice-president of Dial and Delacorte. Now, he works on his own, helping publishers and book clubs dispose of their overstock. Louie is well loved because of his jokes and stories—or in spite of them, (and I am not sure which). He is an old friend of Igor Kropotkin who enjoys Louis's visits as much as I do.

From Harper's comes Zeb Burgess who cheerfully takes punishment from us when his books don't come in on time. Like most of the men, he is not above hand delivering stacks of books on demand. Little, Brown's man is Joe Consolino—a serious, no-nonsense, mature man who always gives a straight answer. We look forward to the visits of Bev Chaney and Frank Dyckman from

Houghton Mifflin. They want to know how their books are doing, but they have never pressured us in any way. Frank Dyckman gave me *Even Cowgirls Get the Blues*, a Houghton Mifflin novel. The book did not become a best-seller, but I enjoyed reading it and shall never forget that Frank included a pale blue T-shirt (even sent the right size) with the book. Written on the shirt was the book's title. I promised I would wear it, and I do, when I ride my bike or rake leaves. Perhaps one day I'll wear it to work.

Stuart Hirsch of Simon & Schuster ambles into Scribner's in a most casual manner and says, "Have *I* got a book for *you*! and most likely he has. Like all the sales reps, he reads the books before he sells them, and he shares his enthusiasm with us. Whenever Eddie Ponger of Holt, Rinehart & Winston comes to mind I think of the day he came in to announce *Fear of Flying* by Erica Jong. He didn't know how it would do anymore than we did, but he stirred our curiosity sufficiently to have several of us read it. That success story is well known. Something is about to happen when Eddie shows up smiling.

Ed Johnston of Doubleday is so much a part of the lovely cocktail parties his company sponsors, how can we not welcome him with open arms? Morrow's newcomer, Don Patterson fits very well into the group of honored visitors. "What would you like to read?" asks Don, and within two hours he will return with books for us in a special Morrow tote bag.

When I think of Mike Maynard of Lippincott, I remember the day I opened a copy of *Publishers Weekly*, the trade magazine for book-sellers and publishers, and

With A Book in My Hand

there was a two-page spread of Lippincott books, with Mike showing them off. He was the perfect man for the ad—white-haired, youthful, smiling, handsome, and impeccably dressed, but I guess he still prefers to be their sales rep.

Walter Oakley, of Norton, who offered me so much support when I made a short speech at a Publisher's Advertising Club luncheon on the subject "Who Buys Books and Why," often asks as he presents a new book, "What do you think of the price?" He listens to our response. He is wise enough to know that the book-seller is a pretty good judge of how the customers will react to the price of a book.

The representative for Knopf and Random House is Howard Treeger. I think we love Howard because he pretends to be shocked if we say something off-color. It's a great act, and he knows that we are on to him, but this is his charm.

Mind you, every one of these men has a delicious sense of humor. Their jokes make our day.

When Toby Wherry of Coward McCann and Putnam arrived recently sporting a new, handsome, leather carrying case, I said, "Sure, it's darn good looking, but I'm always distressed by the heavy bags of books you fellows carry when you make your rounds. I am waiting for the day when you all mount your bags on roller skate wheels."

These gentlemen are some of the most decent men I have ever met. Bar none.

Celia Summer

Although I have always loved the outdoors, I knew that working in the store at Scribner's would leave me little time for the outdoor exercise I crave. Consequently, I became chief gardener, hedge-cutter, and general caretaker of my sister's lawn. She lives in a large Gothic-style house diagonally across the street from my apartment. Her property is forty by a hundred feet and the house is recessed, leaving a substantial front yard and lots of work. I have found the work both relaxing and ideal exercise.

In the winter, I shovel the snow from her driveway and walk, in autumn I rake leaves. This puttering through each season adds a pleasant touch to my "city-dweller" life.

Occasionally, children in the neighborhood will help with the weeding, and then I reward them with ice-cream cones or cookies and music. During work breaks, I play the accordion with a repertoire that includes "Farmer in the Dell" and other such tunes. When the children and I are having our fun on the street, no one interferes. And, no matter how cold the weather or how tedious the work may be, I am usually joined by the same group of good friends.

I will not deny that in the beginning I seduced them into friendship by leading a sidewalk bike trip many times around the block. Whatever prompted me to do that is the same part of me which still glances occasionally at the

With A Book in My Hand

Babar series, or *A Wrinkle in Time*, or *Dr. Seuss* and *Peanuts* when there is a quiet moment in the store.

Two weeks ago, Jürgen Stöhr, Sibylle's husband, came to New York on business. We were supposed to "rendezvous," but Jürgen could not make it, and so he had a messenger deliver a bottle of wine to me with his apologies.

Then I received the following letter from Sibylle enclosed in a package with a bottle of perfume and a paisley shawl.

My very dear friend Celia,
That was terribly sad that you and Jürgen could not get together. He was very sorry indeed. He had some home-made jam with him from me to you. I am almost a jam-manufacturer. Of course, he left the jam in the hotel and forgot all about it! I am very sorry because you keep sending me these marvellous books and now you did not get the jam and no kiss from Jürgen either. What a shame, but we might come together to New York next year, and then we will make up for it and talk constantly with each other for three hours non-stop!!! Thank you so much for the book about

India (*Freedom at Midnight*). You even gave me your own copy to keep? Lapierre has a very nice hand-writing and a very nice looking fellow too!

Yesterday, two more advance reading copies came. I feel so ashamed. I wish you could read German. There are such good books since the Book Fair in Frankfurt. If you come across a book called *La Storia* by Elsa Morante, please read it. It should come out in your country next year—it is the biggest seller in Italy since Lampedusa's *The Leopard*. I have not started *Lovers and Tyrants*. I think I will first finish *Freedom at Midnight* and then I will stop breast-feeding Philipp because it takes away such a lot of strength and then I lack the concentration to read much, but winter is coming, and I am very much looking forward to all the goodies you sent me. Jürgen read *The Hamlet Warning* and thanks you very much. He found it thrilling. He brought back a copy of *Vogue*—October issue—and there was a very good review of *Lovers and Tyrants*.

At the moment, there is a lot of talk in Düsseldorf about *Fear of Flying* by Erica Jong. Of course, I am very sophisticated—thanks to you. I read it long ago, and was able to talk about it in an impressive way. You thought it very funny as I remember you writing to me. In a way, I think people think it funny or amusing or shocking or whatever because it has its fair amount of four-letter words as you call it. I just think the whole

With A Book in My Hand

thing is a terrific put-on to make it sell better. It is a pity really because the layers of put-on obscenity hide some good and sensitive remarks and reflections about the problems men and women have in living and loving together. They celebrate the author as a feminist, a liberated female. I do not at all share this opinion. I would say she is extremely dependent on men and as this, in some ways, is a very private book, pepped up for sales with some so-called dirty language, she, in her private life, must be a bit screwed up (or badly screwed if you want my opinion) because if it's good, one talks about it like good food, the sun, natural things, but one does not try to verbalize sex in this amount. It is "ersatz"—do you understand, Celia?

I suppose I use my thorough fill of four-letter words weekly. It is normal and healthy to have a verbal outlet once in a while—it does not amuse me nor shock me at all. I remember you laughing at the beginning about the use of some words in my daily conversation. Maybe, therefore, the book amused you. Please tell me.

I enclose a shawl for you. It is now very much the fashion over here, Yves Saint Laurent, I think, initiated it, but in Bavaria, they have been draping these shawls around their shoulders for centuries! It shall keep you warm and glamorous this winter—my dear friend. The perfume is made by my uncle.

Love and kisses from
Sibylle, Jürgen, and Philipp

Celia Summer

Several weeks ago, I was invited to read a book that Quadrangle Books was planning to publish early in 1977. A heavy box of typewritten pages was delivered to me on a Friday afternoon. The book was entitled *Wanted!* by Howard Blum. The subject was the tracking down of Nazi criminals still living in America. I started to read it that evening. Almost immediately, I felt a compulsion to go on and on. The compulsion turned into total absorption with the result that I read unceasingly until 3 A.M. that morning, when I could no longer keep my eyes open.

Needless to say, I finished the book on Saturday. Aware that Quadrangle wanted to know my reaction as soon as possible, I put my reaction down on paper minutes after I read the final pages. I was filled with passion and wrote:

Wanted is a highly disturbing, incredible and important book. More than that, it is inspiring too, in the sense that we learn that there are still dedicated men—men of decent morality who will go to the ends of the earth in search of truth and justice. It is a hair-raising revelation of immense proportion—a challenge to all decent Americans to open their eyes—to take a clear look at our strange, twisted laws and corruption in full bloom.

Perhaps, what is more extraordinary is that the

With A Book in My Hand

author, a man under thirty, is capable of capturing the entire impact of Hitler's world with a comprehension one might expect from an elder statesman and with the guts of a giant.

I was flattered, indeed, that Quadrangle chose to use my quote on the front of the prepublication edition of the book that was mailed out to their sales representatives throughout the United States.

It would be useless to try to analyze the reasons behind a "fighting relationship." It is a combination of affection, respect, and a spirit of play.

I had it with Louise Boyer, I have it with Josie Engel, and above all with Marc Connelly. It's been going on for a long time in the book store and people around us would certainly misconstrue our relationship, if they were witness to our comic bickering. It reached a peak just the other night.

I was happily on my way to a cocktail party at Emily Kimbrough's to celebrate her new book *Better Than Oceans*. I came into a large, beautiful room—logs in the fireplace were blazing, my favorite drink, a Bloody Mary, was handed to me. There was a feeling of of warmth that pervaded the entire setting.

Celia Summer

Since Harper's published Miss Kimbrough's book, the company was well-represented by Zeb Burgess, Joan Kahn, and Mr. and Mrs. Cass Canfield. Ever since *Our Hearts Were Young and Gay*, I cannot think of Emily Kimbrough without Cornelia Otis Skinner, and of course, Miss Skinner was there too. All of a sudden, Marc Connelly ambled in and announced that he would have a vodka martini.

"Oh, my God," I exclaimed, "what are you doing here?"

"*Au contraire*," he responded belligerently, "since when have you, a book clerk, moved up to the higher echelons of society?"

"You might as well accept the fact of my existence outside the Scribner Book Store," I replied with phony indignation.

He made clucking sounds with his tongue pretending to indicate his horror at meeting me outside the usual milieu. We agreed to a temporary truce for the evening, and in deference to his age, I leaned over to kiss his cheek.

Toward the end of the party, Mr. Connelly asked me, in a tone which indicated he might escort me home, where I lived.

"I live in Brooklyn," I stated proudly.

He threw up his hands in disgust, and certainly I can understand his reaction. Most Manhattanites regard Brooklyn as the end of the world, and so I called out "*arrivederci*" and waved goodbye to my literary friends.

With A Book in My Hand

There have been some changes since I began to write about my friends.

Sibylle and Jürgen Stöhr of Dusseldorf have produced a fine little boy named Philipp Michael. A week after he was born, his proud father bought a football for his son, the athlete.

Our Joe Dennehy died, and with his passing went the dulcet tones of the commander-in-chief of the Scribner basement. I did not realize how much I would miss that volatile temper which covered up a soft heart—no more the supervisor of our Christmas parties, and the voice that burst out into song when there were a couple of drinks under his belt.

Sir John Wheeler-Bennett is no longer alive. Never again will he drop in to brighten our days. I remember one of his favorite stories about a large book shop in London. He had overheard a customer ask for the new Alistair Cooke book. The young novice responded to the request by pointing and stating, "All the books on the subject are over there in the cookbook section."

Mary Hemingway finished the story of her life with Mr. Hemingway. She finally settled on the title, *How it Was*. She came into Scribner's the other day to do some autographing. Her first question to me after we greeted each other was, "Did you find a title for your book?"

"Yes, I did."

Celia Summer

"What is it?"

"*With A Book in My Hand.*"

"Sounds good," she said approvingly." I'll come in to buy an autographed copy."

I wonder what it will feel like—this business of being an author.

In 1975, a slim, attractive man from the Midde East who carried himself with the quiet sureness of a diplomat asked me to help him select a fair amount of new books (those I felt would be worth reading), so that he could ship them home to a suburb outside London. My adrenalin began to work. I love to suggest books I have enjoyed especially when I have free rein. He accepted my choices without reservation. After we stacked them, he asked, "May I use my American Express Card?"

"Sure thing," I replied

Above a certain amount, it is mandatory that we call American Express for authorization. To my amazement, I found that Amex called London to check his credit.

Unlike many customers, this man showed no annoyance. On the contrary, he seemed particularly amused at the checking system. Patiently, he waited, and as he did so, a young man approached me asking if we had a certain back title book on finance. I didn't think so. My patient customer turned to him, "I have a copy at home. If you give me your name and address, I would be happy to send it on to you."

I looked with surprise but said nothing. I learned later that the man fulfilled his promise because the young man came back to Scribner's to tell me; he found it incredulous that a total stranger could be so kind.

Before the gentleman from the Midde East left, he asked, "Is there anything you would like me to send to you from London?"

Shyly, I said, "Thank you, but I cannot think of anything at the moment." We said goodbye.

Only a few weeks ago, he entered the store again, this time with his pretty wife and I was so happy to see him.

"Have you had your lunch yet?" he asked.

"Yes, I have."

"In that case, why don't we get down to the business of choosing some good books."

This time the stack was a tall one (twelve books) and I learned, as we talked, that their son was a student at Oxford.

"Do you think your son would deliver a message to a friend of mine at All Soul's College?" I asked.

"Of course," he replied.

"Well just tell him to send my love to A. L. Rowse."

"No problem," he said. "We will oblige." Then he added, "Whenever you feel a book is appropriate for me, will you be good enough to call me collect in London or at home."

He proceeded to give me both numbers as I stood there speechless.

Celia Summer

"Furthermore," he went on, "I want you to think of something—anything you would like for me to send to you."

He stated it in such a way that I felt if I asked for a small car, or a ten-speed bike, he would think nothing of it.

"I'll think about it and I shall write to you when I decide," I said quite honestly.

"Very good, Miss Summer—it will be my pleasure."

All the while, his wife stood by with an amused look on her face. She seemed to be enjoying the whole thing. We all shook hands and said goodbye.

That night, I felt as if I wanted to write to him, and did so, saying that I was having trouble that past week shopping for a good-looking blazer—well tailored—in my size, and I'd be grateful to get one, provided I could pay for it plus shipping charges. I sent the letter airmail.

Two days later, my new friends reappeared. I'd thought they'd left for London.

"I called home," he said, "and my son read me your letter. Now, what is this all about—this blazer—what size do you need? What are your measurements?"

I had lost over ten pounds recently and I was no longer sure of my size. We all thought for a couple of minutes.

"Do you have an old blazer we can take back to London, and then we will send both back to you?" he asked.

"Of course—that's a great idea—I've a summer jacket that will do just fine," I said with relief.

"Excellent idea," he agreed.

With A Book in My Hand

Again, the gentleman and his wife came back the following day to pick up my old blazer.

"I am on my way to an international monetary conference in the Far East, my wife is going home to London and she will do the shopping for you. Now, you want, in short, an elegant blazer," he said.

"Yes, I do."

By this time, I'd fallen in love with him, and did not dare to speak of money or the cost involved. His wife nodded approval of the whole deal.

"May I kiss him goodbye?" I asked her.

"Of course," she replied.

On October 26, 1976, I received a cablegram as follows;

YOUR BLAZER SHALL REACH AMERICA WITH MRS. JOHNSON SHE IS REACHING NEW YORK IN A WEEK OR TEN DAYS AND SHE WILL SEND THE BLAZER WITH HER CHAUFFEUR STOP HAVE RECEIVED SOME OF THE BOOKS THANK YOU FOR EVERYTHING

LOVE

On the tenth day, I called Mrs. Johnson. She had the blazer for me at her home. I suggested that I pick it up, since parking on Fifth Avenue is prohibitive these days. We had a date for 4 P.M. I arrived promptly, with a book in my hand for her. I thought if she was gracious enough to carry a package for me all the way from London, the least I could do would be to bring her my favorite book of the moment, *Lovey* by Mary MacCracken. It is a

Celia Summer

wonderful book about a remarkable teacher who works with disturbed children. This touching story is equal to four text books on the subject of handicapped youngsters.

Mrs. Johnson and I shared some delicious wine, as she told me about the time she and her husband spent with my Middle East friend and his wife in London. She agreed he is one of the most charming men that she, too, has ever met.

Then she handed the package to me. The jacket emerged. It is a four-pocketed velvet blazer trimmed with black grosgrain ribbon. It is the most beautiful blazer I have ever had.

I managed to get back uptown on time to attend a party for Margaret Truman in the library of the St. Regis Hotel. Her book, *Women of Courage*, had just been published by Morrow. I checked my coat, but I couldn't let go of the blazer for fear of losing it and so I kept it alongside me throughout the evening. Meanwhile, Faith Cross and I mingled with the guests, and I managed to wring a promise from the former President's daughter to come to Scribner's to autograph her book. I expect she will, and we will be happy to have her.

I called London to thank my friend for the gift. He said, "I've kept your old blazer in case you want another one." I couldn't answer.

With A Book in My Hand

After Thanksgiving, Christmas wreaths were hung on the walls in the book store, and trees were placed in the windows; it was warm inside, cold outside, and above all the pleasant sound of fine music was gently heard throughout the store. I couldn't believe my ears. The sound of music in the Scribner Book Store was something totally new for us. The whole spirit of Christmas permeated the place and there were all the signs that we were ready for the deluge of customers. It was my tenth Christmas at Scribner's.

At 10 A.M. that Friday morning, I was called to the phone in the book store with the announcement, "London is calling you, Miss Summer."

I knew it had to be my Middle East friend.

"I am not one for writing letters, and so I've called to thank you for sending me *Raise the Titanic*. I enjoyed it very much," he announced enthusiastically.

"I'm so pleased," I purred.

"By the way, what kind of tweed jacket would you like?" he asked.

"Oh," I replied with some shock, "just a sport jacket, tweed or suede or a combination of both!"

"Well, I will let my wife do the shopping since you were so pleased with her last purchase," he said.

"That's a wonderful idea," I agreed, "she has superb taste."

"I want to tell you," he added, "we will be in New York December 20th before we go on to Florida. Perhaps we can have lunch together."

"I would love it and I want to be sure about the date

Celia Summer

so I can wear my black velvet blazer and show you how well it looks on me."

"Very well," he said, "we will see you soon."

When I returned to my desk, I received the usual amount of kidding that anyone receives when she acts casual about receiving an overseas call. But I was as smug as could be.

When the Christmas season starts, many things happen that give me a sense of accelerated pace, excitement, and stimulation. I begin to feel this in September as the books start to pour into our basement in large quantities from the publishers. There will be parties for authors, and people I haven't seen for months will suddenly appear with long shopping lists.

A dinner party for Alex Haley, author of *Roots* was an example of a publishing party more festive possibly because the holiday was approaching. And then there was a party for Taylor Caldwell held at my favorite place, the suite of rooms at the Doubleday building on Fifth Avenue and 53rd Street. The Scribner group paid its respects to Miss Caldwell, who was pleased to see us. She reminded us that in her early days as an author, Scribner's was her publisher. The living rooms of the Doubleday suite at 53rd Street and Fifth Avenue are comfortable

With A Book in My Hand

and homey with soft chairs, couches—the whole setting is an invitation to make yourself at home and stay a while. We always stay to the end of the Doubleday parties.

Just before I left for Taylor Caldwell's party, a tall willowy, pretty blond woman asked me if I had a copy of *Lovers and Tyrants*. She needed the book for a friend in the hospital. Like a puppy who can sense a friend, I can smell an author yards away.

"You're not Francine du Plessix Gray, are you?"

"I am."

Regretfully, we did not have her book in stock that day and I must admit that Ms. Gray is the only author I've ever met who was not irritated by the fact that the book had not arrived from the publisher, though I knew it was on its way.

"Look," I suggested, "if you give me a call within two days, the book will probably be here, and then it would be fun for you to come in and autograph the books." (I was also thinking of Christmas and our customers who love inscribed books).

Our shipment arrived the following day so that when Simon & Schuster's publicity department called, I was able to say, "Yes, please have Mrs. Gray come in."

Like most authors, she was also worried about the reviewers and what they would say. I adored the book having read it before in proof copy. Therefore with genuine conviction and appreciation of her talent, I reassured her, "Don't worrry, everything will be all right."

Of course, her success is now history.

She was on her way out of the store about noontime,

Celia Summer

but she turned, bent over to kiss me. I can envision *Lovers and Tyrants* finding the same devoted readers as Colette, Simone de Beauvoir, and Proust. Francine du Plessix Gray has thoughtful things to say about women in a man's world.

The publishing house of Charles Scribner's Sons has been holding weekly seminars in the board room on the eighth floor of the Scribner Building for members of various departments in order to familiarize everyone with the systems used by each section to achieve its goals.

My boss, Igor Kropotkin, invited me to join him at a seminar so that we could answer questions on how the Scribner Book Store functions. As it is difficult to refuse Igor anything, I agreed.

By morning of the day scheduled for the seminar, I was as nervous as could be. Anne Sullivan, who is in charge of copyrights, had arranged the seminar. She came down to see me that morning. She inspected me from head to foot and said, "You are suitably dressed."

"What do you mean, about how I'm dressed?" I began to doubt myself.

"Well, NBC news will be there," said Anne with a straight face.

"Oh, I think I'll die now," I cried out.

With A Book in My Hand

"No, you'll be fine—I'll hold your hand before we start."

Later in the morning, dear, sweet Mary Semple, who is head of personnel, came into the book store. I foolishly asked her if she would come to the seminar.

"Oh, I'll try, Ceil—I think Channel 2 news will be there!"

Then I was totally paralyzed.

The seminar started and I saw no TV equipment. I felt much more relaxed. I've yet to think of a punishment to fit Anne's and Mary's crime.

There were twelve in our audience. Igor explained the problems of the rising prices on hardcover books. He added that we had increased our paperbacks so that people will have broader choices. He also pointed out, in a response to a question, that the retail mark-up of prices is in no way comparable to the large mark-up of clothing, for example. However, we have the privilege of returning books to publishers when they don't sell at all.

I discussed best-sellers; how they develop, how word-of-mouth helps, and how we increase our orders in relation to demand. As for our method of window displays, I explained, decisions are made on the basis of season or holidays. Igor informed our audience that we do not call in a professional to decorate the windows. Our co-worker, John P. Stuehr, writer and actor, has a beautiful flair for doing the windows each week. His taste is impeccable, his combination of colors is most attractive, and he does all this quietly and competently.

Something interesting occurred while my "boss" and I

Celia Summer

conducted the seminar. A rapport developed between Igor and me which produced much laughter in the audience. His humor is subtle and dry. Mine is less inhibited, and I found myself telling silly little anecdotes that could only occur in a large book shop. The hour and a half passed faster than I thought it would. I am relieved it is over, but I have to admit it was fun.

Several years ago, while he was still a student at Princeton, young Charles Scribner III spent a summer working in the book store to get the feel of what it was like to be in the retail book trade. We became friends. Charlie is an attractive, wholesome young man with a deep interest in books. Now, of course, he is a member of the firm of Charles Scribner's Sons.

He confessed to me that he was responsible for pulling me into the seminar. He said to the senior members of the publishing house, "If you really want to learn what goes on in the book store, invite Celia Summer along with Mr. Kropotkin to help conduct the seminar."

In spite of my stage fright, I thank Charlie for his kind words. I also received the following comment from Pat Luca who works well with Norman Kotker, history editor of Scribner's. She wrote:

Emotional Response—by Pat Luca

I walked into the board room on Monday, November 15th, prepared for "Marketing IV—Igor Kropotkin," and was pleasantly surprised to

With A Book in My Hand

see Celia Summer seated next to the scheduled speaker of the day. I knew I was in for an interesting session, to say the least, and I settled back into my seat to watch the action.

When I came to Scribner's almost two years ago, I was given a sound bit of advice. I was told that, whenever it was necessary to go down to the book store, I must seek out Celia for information on anything. I quickly learned that it was a piece of advice to be taken seriously. I think that any regular customer would agree with me when I say that Celia *is* Scribner's Book Store. With that little twinkle in her eye, she is full of surprises, and always has a kind word to say.

Getting back to November 15th ... I wish I had gotten it down on tape. The interplay between Celia and her "boss," as she refers to him, was priceless. Mr. Kropotkin, who is obviously quite fond of Celia, seemed glad to have her along. Celia's spontaneity, her fits of laughter, and her adorable anecdotes were a delightful buffer to Mr. Kropotkin's ever-present dry sense of humor. He proceeded to talk about the workings of the book store, only to be interrupted time and again by his admiring employee. Running a book store involves solid judgment, expertise, intuition, and countless other qualities. The mutual respect and admiration displayed by this team contribute to making the book store what it is.

By the way, anyone who hasn't met Celia is

Celia Summer

really missing what Scribner's Book Store is all about. She's a joy.

I was totally shocked when I watched and listened recently to a television program called "Eye on New York." There before my eyes, was a picture of a small, average town on Long Island called *Island Trees*. This small community seems to be split in two over the fact that the high-school library banned the novel, *The Fixer*, by Bernard Malamud.

I couldn't believe this. It couldn't be happening here so close to home—yet it was. I listened to heated arguments among parents and between the high-school principal and parents. I kept remembering Ray Bradbury's *Fahrenheit 451*, the story of the burning of books that takes place sometime in the future. I was so distressed that I immediately wrote to Mr. Malamud (a good customer of mine) asking for his reactions to the current situation on Long Island.

The banning of books is a terribly vital issue to people in and out of the book business. It is a very sensitive area, and as long as I have been at the Scribner Book Store, I know that we have carried books from all responsible publishers—impartially.

I enclose herein Mr. Malamud's response to my letter.

With A Book in My Hand

Dear Celia,

    I didn't see the TV program you refer to but my feeling is that you can't melt nuts in honey: you can't reason about books with bigots. It's best to let the courts deal with them. In one case, recently, it was decided that school libraries must be treated with the same respect other libraries are. They can't be the subject of depredations by bigots. The ACLU is suing to have the books censored by the Island Trees School Board returned to the library shelves. I'm certain they will be.

    Good luck on your book!

Yours,
Bernard Malamud

A number of years ago, one of my favorite customers Barbara Brubaker, a highly sophisticated and well-traveled lady, confessed to me that her favorite of all writers is E. B. White. Since I, too, shared her enthusiasm, we had many long-winded discussions about the effect he had on us. Barbara had read everything E. B. White had written, and she was particularly interested in knowing whether Mr. White had anything in the works.

"Write to him," I suggested.

"I couldn't think of it," she replied shyly.

Celia Summer

"Why not? I know he will answer you," I said.

Well, she was such a "reluctant dragon" about the whole thing, that I took it upon myself to act as the go-between.

Some time later, Barbara rushed into Scribner's to tell me her good news. She had received a response From Mr. White.

In November 1976, *Letters of E. B. White* was published by Harper & Row. On page 573, Mrs. Max Brubaker and I are immortalized.

Sarasota, Fla.
December 28, 1968

Dear Mrs. Brubaker:

Celia Summer, of the Scribner Book Store, says you want to know whether I have a book in the making. It is very heartening to know that somebody cares about this.

All writing men have a book in the making; the only question is, what happens. I cannot at this point tell you, or forecast, what will happen. I have in my bedroom a rather heavy, legal-size envelope, and as near as I can make out, it contains about two-thirds of the manuscript of a book. I am 69 years old. It's that last third that I wonder about.

Thanks for the inquiry.

Sincerely,
E. B. White

With A Book in My Hand

Since I had a need to explain how this all came about, I wrote to Mr. White for permission to use the preceding letter in my book. The following was his reply:

November 22, 1976

Dear Miss Summer:

I have no objection to your quoting the letter on page 573. I forget what it says and can't look it up because Harper hasn't got round to sending me any books, and I'm too stubborn to go to a book store and buy one. Good luck with your book.

Yrs,
E. B. White

When I was invited to make a short speech at the publisher's advertisers luncheon, I boldly assented. I had never made a speech before. The subject was "Who Buys Books and Why." My boss, Igor Kropotkin, felt I could do it, and I was flattered by his confidence in me.

I thought about it, wrote and rewrote, and finally managed to put together some thoughts on the subject. But each time I envisioned myself in front of an audience, I recoiled in terror. I tried to back out, but it was too late. I had committed myself. I invited my sister

Celia Summer

along so that she could pick up the pieces when I fell apart. As my name was announced, my heart palpitated like the sound of the cannons in Tschaikovsky's 1812 Overture.

I stood up, began to speak, and suddenly it was all right because I blurted out, "Forgive me—I'm scared stiff." The audience smiled with quiet compassion, but more than that, Walter Oakley of Norton was sitting there, and I could focus on him—he has been such a good friend for years. Then I went on with the following speech:

> When Mr. David Cather's secretary called me at the Scribner Book Store and asked, "What is your position there?"
>
> "No particular position ... I'm just in charge of history, archaeology, anthropology, American Indians, current affairs, and the best-seller table and I also sell books," I replied.
>
> What with Barbara Walters, Gene Shalit, Anatole Broyard, and Martha Dane and all the literary mishmash that goes on in the morning on radio and TV ... it's a miracle that we get to work at all on time.
>
> Recently, a woman approached me at our staid emporium.
>
> "Where," she asked, "might I find *The Joy of Sex?*"
>
> "You will find the joy of sex on our balcony." I never saw her come down again. So when a very

With A Book in My Hand

nice man asked me where he could find *The Great Bridge*, I automatically said, "You'll find the great bridge over the East River."

The book-seller is the intermediary between the writer and the public. We must discover what the customer wants, and then connect the need to the appropriate book. There is no trick to this. You must know and love the world of books and you must also have the desire to fill the needs of the book-reading people. If I were presumptuous, I might say that it is possible for me to be an advance agent for culture.

If you raise the question, Why do people buy books today? I am compelled to answer you with a quote from a bibliophile named Richard de Bury, born in the year 1287. I quote:

> Books are masters who instruct us without rods or ferules, without word or anger, without bread or money. If you approach them, they do not hide; if you blunder, they do not scold; if you are ignorant, they do not laugh at you.

At Scribner's, books are purchased, for the most part, by mature, sophisticated, and civilized people with a variety of interests depending upon their vocations and hobbies. Areas of interest in books are mutable because there are vogues in reading as flexible as styles in apparel. At the moment, there is a plethora of publications about the stock market, the occult, psychiatry, ecological catastrophes, gourmet cooking, and the third sex!

Thomas Carlyle once said that biography is the only true history. If a man lives only one life ... confined to one part of the universe, then in order to broaden and enrich his life, he must do so by learning about other lives from biographies of people who have risen above mediocrity into greatness and success. Through the magic of the writer, we can peer into the private and public life of an individual. Good biography portrays the subject from without and from within and we are there to see it all put together, in short, we become "peeping-toms" and unashamedly so.

Great writing is timeless; for example, I must quote from *The Blithedale Romance* written in 1852, by Nathaniel Hawthorne.

The heroine speaks:

> It is my belief, yes and my prophecy, should I die before it happens ... that when my sex shall achieve its rights, there will be ten eloquent women where there is now one eloquent man. Thus far, no woman in the world has ever once spoken out her whole heart and her whole mind. The mistrust and disapproval of the vast bulk of society throttles us with two gigantic hands at our throats! We mumble a few

With A Book in My Hand

weak words, and leave a thousand better ones unsaid. It is with the living voice alone that she can compel the world to recognize the light of her intellect and the depth of her heart.

What I have read to you needs no comment save that we seem to hear the voice of Margaret Fuller stilled for a hundred and twenty years through the instrumentality of Hawthorne's genius as a writer.

Also, consider this statement spoken by a female physician in the novel *Ann Vickers* by Sinclair Lewis written in the 1920s.

As an unofficial officer of the state, Ann, I must make it clear that abortion is a crime. Speaking as a physician, I advise you against having an abortion. It is abnormal and dangerous. You may never be able to bear a second child. And every woman ought to bear a child, if only for the sake of functioning properly. But, speaking as a woman, I strongly advise you to have the abortion and keep your mouth shut about it afterward. As long as men and what's worse, the female women that let themselves be governed by men's psychology have made our one peculiar function, child-

Celia Summer

bearing, somehow indecent and exceptional, we have to fight back and be realistic about it, and lie and conceal as much as they do. So, I give you my word, I've only done five abortions. In each case I thought the patient was more valuable to the world than what I am pleased to call my honor as a physician and a citizen.

And so, reading serves many purposes. People want to learn, to be inspired, to expand their visions and awareness, to understand the world around them, to travel in time, to gain insight into themselves and into others, to compare, to escape into fantasy, to be entertained, to be beguiled, to have fun, to share experiences, and to discuss them with others. It then becomes a communal activity.

Consider, if you will, the how-to books:

> How not to fall off a mountain
> How to be a female eunuch
> How to talk to practically
>   anybody about anything
> How to eat and grow thin
> How to cope with a neurotic dog

I believe book buying is not only a beautiful addiction, but also represents a lifelong love affair with all that is the best and the brightest in the

With A Book in My Hand

minds and hearts of men and women throughout history.

And speaking about *The Best and the Brightest*, the book is a good example of how a fine piece of writing bursts out into a flourishing best-seller. The trick was to have it in abundance throughout the 1972 Christmas season.

I am proud to say we were never without the book from its inception until this very moment. The reviews were great, people told each other, and among many other things, it was a delectable dish of high-class gossip.

Need I belabor any longer the value and relevance of reading? Certainly, not to this audience. It has been said and bears repeating that the collective education of the world depends upon books. They are the sole instruments of transmitting and perpetuating thought. Joseph Addison (of Addison and Steele) said it well: "Books are the legacies that genius leaves to mankind to be delivered down from generation to generation as presents to those that are yet unborn."

There are certain rules I've conjured up over the years for dealing with book buyers ... they are as follows:

1. Be careful not to inject derogatory remarks about a book. The customer could be a relative of or the author himself.

Celia Summer

2. For people who are non-readers, it's best to offer a gossip book, for example *Tracy and Hepburn, The Moon's a Balloon*, or a book about Howard Hughes.

3. You cannot force a book upon a customer. There can only be a "friendly persuasion" and an informed enthusiasm.

4. Keep a distance. It is dangerous to make any personal remarks whatsoever. You might stir up a hornet's nest. In short, there is considerable need for diplomacy in every area of the book world.

I wish it didn't take so long to learn!

I sent a copy of my speech to Shirley Hazzard and her husband Francis Steegmuller. His reply is the stuff that makes this whole book business the best of all possible worlds.

11 March 1973

Dear Celia,

I am moved by your wise and witty "Who Buys Books and Why." You speak from the heart and mind and from a whole experience that is itself a study of human affairs. After we left you

With A Book in My Hand

both (Francis Hayden and me) the other day, we talked about the favorable transformation wreaked on one's view of this world by such an encounter as we'd just had with you two: with those, in fact, who believe in human quality and whose very belief extends human possibilities. There is so much of this large view in your speech ... and I particularly like knowing the beautiful quotation from Richard de Bury.

I've now given the speech to Francis and I know he'll have as much pleasure in it as I do. Thank you! for remembering this and taking the trouble to send it.

Now—another compliment for you. A fan letter from a kind reader tells me that her husband bought the book the *Defeat of an Ideal* at Scribner's where "he was taken care of by a charming lady who surely knows and cares about books."

Speaking for authors, let me say that we rejoice that this is so! With very warmest regards from us both, and again with thanks—

Most sincerely,
Shirley H.